Endorsements

"This is a terrific book. It is engaging and should be enormously helpful to anyone wanting to improve the efficiency and functioning of their healthcare enterprise. It clearly lays out why and how to implement Lean in healthcare settings."

Richard D. Krugman, MD
Vice Chancellor for Health Affairs and Dean
University of Colorado School of Medicine

"An inspiring book by one of the nation's leaders in health systems change that not only chronicles one major institution's transformation but empowers readers to follow suit."

Sara Rosenbaum, JD
Harold and Jane Hirsh Professor
George Washington University
School of Public Health and Health Services
Department of Health Policy

"For years, discussions of the broken US healthcare system have been long on diagnosis and short on solutions. *The Lean Prescription: Powerful Medicine for Our Ailing Healthcare System* aims to fix that. By mixing explanation, thought exercises and real-life examples, Gabow and Goodman provide a thoughtful and accessible introduction to the discipline of Lean and its application within healthcare systems. By grounding the book in their real-life experience, they paint a clear and realistic picture of the commitment necessary, the enthusiasm and empowerment engendered and the exceptional results Denver Health achieved for its patients and its staff. For any leader who's looking for a serious approach—not a silver bullet—to making their system work better for all stakeholders, this book holds a powerful message."

Risa Lavizzo-Mourey, MD, MBA
President and CEO
Robert Wood Johnson Foundation

"*The Lean Prescription: Powerful Medicine for Our Ailing Healthcare System* is a prescription for excellence. It vaults to the top of the management must-read list. Patty Gabow charts a way forward for every health executive working to achieve breakthrough results for every patient."

Bruce Siegel, MD, MPH
President & CEO
America's Essential Hospitals

"Dr. Gabow demonstrates in *The Lean Prescription: Powerful Medicine for Our Ailing Healthcare System* how a CEO can change a culture and deliver massive improvement in healthcare delivery, including over $190 million in financial benefit over seven years, through disciplined Lean leadership."

George Koenigsaecker
President of Lean Investments, LLC

"Patty Gabow and Philip Goodman have succinctly captured the enormous power of Lean management as applied to healthcare. In the process they provide exercises which can deepen the reader's grasp of concepts and tools. Notably, the accomplishments they document have been achieved in safety net institutions—a challenge and inspiration to everyone who works in such settings: even with constrained resources we can get better outcomes for our patients by systematically reducing waste and improving reliability."

Mark Smith, MD
Retired, President and CEO
California HealthCare Foundation

"Dr. Gabow's amazing process improvements at Denver Health Medical Center were the inspiration for our own journey with Lean techniques. Her new book can teach specific techniques to other leaders in the medical field on how to improve their delivery of healthcare, with the focus on where it should be: on patients and their care. In these pages, Dr. Gabow has offered the great gifts of her experience and wisdom. For those with the will to improve, this book can be their guide."

John Hickenlooper
Governor of Colorado

"If you have any responsibility for any part of the healthcare systems in the United States, your experience and the health of your patients will be better for having read, understood and acted on the clear steps described in this unusual book. Not a treatise, it is a guidebook to take us from the jungle of cost, waste, and confusion to the clarity of efficiency and mission."

Christine Cassel, MD
President and CEO
National Quality Forum

"With Lean, Dr. Gabow applies a concept developed and honed in the private world to public services. Lean's approach empowers workers to eliminate waste, improving quality, and reducing costs. We should embrace this thinking to improve the value of our public organizations."

Senator Michael Bennet
United States Senator from Colorado

"Dr. Gabow and Phil Goodman have thoroughly captured seven years of experience in this engaging and straightforward re-telling of their highly acclaimed Lean transformation of Denver Health. All of us who know and worked closely with Patty appreciate her unparalleled attention to detail and hands-on leadership of her operations as CEO of this magnificent public hospital system. In *The Lean Prescription: Powerful Medicine for Our Ailing Healthcare System* that same Gabow mastery of nuances and the critical elements of transforming a large health system are factually presented, covering not just select clinical areas but the whole enterprise ... as it should be done. Bravo Patty and Phil for your crisp presentation of the why, the how to, and the real results of Lean's impact on Denver Health!"

Marc Hafer
President and CEO, Simpler Consulting

"To non-initiates, Lean can seem alternately intimidating or dull. Patty Gabow has demonstrated its power in action through the results she achieved at Denver Health. Now she has written a readable guide to Lean that will be useful for managers, providers and all who are struggling to make healthcare work. This book is a great way to dive in."

Margaret O'Kane
President
National Committee for Quality Assurance

Patricia A. Gabow MD, MACP • Philip L. Goodman

The Lean Prescription

Powerful Medicine for Our Ailing Healthcare System

CRC Press
Taylor & Francis Group
Boca Raton London New York

CRC Press is an imprint of the
Taylor & Francis Group, an **informa** business

A PRODUCTIVITY PRESS BOOK

CRC Press
Taylor & Francis Group
6000 Broken Sound Parkway NW, Suite 300
Boca Raton, FL 33487-2742

Printed on acid-free paper
Version Date: 20140909

International Standard Book Number-13: 978-1-4822-4638-4 (Hardback)

Library of Congress Cataloging-in-Publication Data

Gabow, Patricia A., author.
   The lean prescription : powerful medicine for our ailing healthcare system / Patricia A. Gabow, Philip L. Goodman.
   p. ; cm.
   Includes bibliographical references and index.
   ISBN 978-1-4822-4638-4 (hardback : alk. paper)
   I. Goodman, Philip L., author. II. Title.
   [DNLM: 1. Delivery of Health Care--economics--United States. 2. Cost Savings--methods--United States. 3. Health Care Costs--United States. 4. Quality of Health Care--United States. W 84 AA1]

RA401.A3
338.4'76151--dc23   2014034111

Visit the Taylor & Francis Web site at
http://www.taylorandfrancis.com

and the CRC Press Web site at
http://www.crcpress.com

To our own families who have given us support,

encouragement, and most of all, love.

To our Denver Health family whose tireless commitment to doing

the right thing has been the inspiration for our Lean journey.

To the millions of patients whose suffering and

resilience made us always want to do better.

Contents

Foreword

It has been my personal and professional good fortune to know Patty Gabow for well over a decade. That included the period when she was first encountering the theory and practice of Lean production, and beginning to see how it might fit Denver Health, the organization that she had led, brilliantly, for years before.

A leader of lesser curiosity and intellect might well have treated the new management method casually, as many have done—trying the "quick study" approach—the "CliffsNotes™" version, delegating the tasks early, moving her own time and attention on to other stuff, and setting up a programmatic office somewhere down the corridor or down the street, out of sight if not completely out of mind.

What I saw was different, and sorely needed in the ranks of healthcare executive leadership and governance. I saw an accomplished executive, who had every apparent right to rest on her considerable laurels, nonetheless begin transformation for real. In retrospect, that is astounding.

When Dr. Gabow began the journey she describes in this book, Denver Health under her guidance was not a floundering struggling place. Far from it. Her managerial skill, clinical vision, political savvy, and dedication to mission had placed her organization at the very front rank of American academic medical centers and, among them, one of the finest examples of a totally integrated healthcare system in the nation. Even though Denver Health was by and large a safety net system with high reliance on Medicaid payment and many patients with no payment source at all, it had under Dr. Gabow turned a positive margin in every single year of her leadership, and had matured an enviable network of community-based primary care clinics without one whit of compromise in the quality and energy of the tertiary flagship hospital. Indeed, by independent metrics, Denver Health had some of the best healthcare quality and outcomes in the entire nation.

Without a burning platform—in fact, starting on a platform most hospital leaders would kill for—what on earth was Patty Gabow thinking? Transform? Why?

It is the mark of a truly great leader, and Dr. Gabow is one, to see beyond the present to the destinations that may lie ahead, and to the icebergs *en route.* Patty is driven by a relentless search for "better" and by a crystal-clear view of realities long before most others see them. I have rarely, if ever, met a person with such a compelling combination of uncomfortable truth-telling and thrilling optimism. She can say, in one breath, both "Wake up! Iceberg ahead!" and "Do you realize what's possible?" and be convincing on both counts.

Patty saw Lean thinking as an important solution in a future most others did not see, and, frankly, mostly still don't. It did not come easy. I remember a phone call with her a year or so after she had begun to use the methods. "We just don't have results yet," she lamented. "This is going to be hard. It's going to take more." A person of lesser skill and optimism would have thrown in the towel, but not Patty. She studied the lessons from her own experience, changed course, drew on expert mentors, and doggedly kept at it. In so doing, she did for the rest of us the hard and essential work of adapting theory and technique to a new context. This dedication found traction in the expert guidance of Patty's coauthor for this book, Phil Goodman, who was the head of the Lean Systems Improvement Department for Denver Health's entire Lean journey, and who oversaw the training of over 250 "Black Belts," coached the entire executive team, and involved 2,000 employees in rapid improvement events.

The results speak volumes about the merit of such diligence. This was no overnight success; it is a decade-long story. But who would expect "transformation" to take less?

Was it worth it? Read on through these pages. Healthcare in this nation is struggling, frankly chaotically, toward the "Triple Aim" articulated by the Institute for Healthcare Improvement: better care for individuals, better health for populations, and lower per capita cost. The stakes are very high. Failure will mean a healthcare system far less ambitious than befits our nation, and one that inevitably offers less to the people who need it the most: the poor, the vulnerable, the marginalized, and people with disabilities.

Here in these pages—and in Denver Health's story—is as close an approximation to the Triple Aim in progress as one can find in America. As hard as this journey has been, it is a shining ray of hope for American healthcare.

Executives and Boards who read this book may feel intimidated. They ought to be. As every accomplished leader in globally competitive industries has discovered (or failed in their mission), the demands of transformation to Lean production and true customer-centered work are relentless, nondelegable, and complicated.

I am reminded repeatedly in this regard of the words I heard first from an accomplished military leader, and have repeated often since: "Strategy is for amateurs; logistics are for professionals." Patty Gabow is a brilliant strategist, largely because she sees the future more clearly than most others do. But, she is also a master logistician, walking her large and important organization through the rough and ragged journey between a great idea for the times and the realization of that idea in the day-to-day lives and work of the place and people she leads.

Now, let's follow.

Donald M. Berwick, MD, MPP
President Emeritus and Senior Fellow
Institute for Healthcare Improvement

Acknowledgments

Denver Health and its executive team, Lean Systems Improvement Department, and many committed employees who embraced Lean and created the journey we are describing.

Simpler Consulting and the Simpler Sensei who taught us much of what we know about Lean and who guided our journey. Without their guidance, Denver Health would have had no meaningful Lean journey. We also thank them for learning with us as they first entered the healthcare space, reflecting wonderful humility.

The Rockefeller Foundation, which provided one of us (Gabow) an academic writing residency at the Rockefeller Foundation Center in Bellagio, Italy. This was valuable time for writing this book.

The Agency for Healthcare Research and Quality that provided the initial grant funding that enabled us to pursue approaches for system transformation and started us on our Lean journey.

The Caring for Colorado Foundation that also provided some initial funding for us to begin our Lean journey.

About the Authors

Patricia A. Gabow, MD, MACP, was CEO of Denver Health from 1992 until her retirement in 2012, initially transforming it from a department of city government to a successful, independent governmental entity and then leading its Lean transformation. Denver Health's Lean effort earned the Shingo Bronze Medallion for Operational Excellence, the first healthcare entity in the world to receive such recognition. Prior to becoming CEO, Dr. Gabow was a practicing nephrologist and academic researcher serving as chief of nephrol-

ogy, director of medical services, and chief medical officer at Denver Health. Dr. Gabow is a member of the Medicaid and CHIP Payment and Access Commission (MACPAC), the Robert Wood Johnson Foundation Board of Trustees, the Institute of Medicine Roundtable on Value and Science Driven Health Care, the National Governors' Association Health Advisory Board, and a senior advisor to Simpler. She is a professor of medicine at the University of Colorado School of Medicine and has authored more than 150 articles and book chapters. She earned her MD degree from the University of Pennsylvania School of Medicine. She has received numerous awards including the AMA Nathan Davis Award for Outstanding Public Servant, the National Healthcare Leadership Award, the David E. Rogers Award from the Association of American Medical Colleges (AAMC), the Health Quality Leader Award from the National Committee for Quality Assurance (NCQA), and was elected to the Association for Manufacturing Excellence for her work in bringing Lean into healthcare.

Philip L. Goodman, MS, RRT, was the director of the Lean Systems Improvement Department at Denver Health, overseeing the Lean facilitators and Lean educational initiatives. In this role he led the operational aspects of the Lean transformation effort, the Black Belt training program, and the Lean Academy at Denver Health. Goodman was employed at Denver Health from 1979 until his retirement in 2013. Prior to directing the Lean Systems Improvement Department, he was the service line administrator for the Department of Medicine and director of respiratory therapy at Denver Health. Goodman is a Denver Health Master Black Belt and a registered respiratory therapist. He earned his master's degree in healthcare administration from Regis University in Denver. Goodman has conducted numerous presentations of Denver Health's Lean transformation effort at the national level.

Introduction

This book grew from my (Patricia Gabow) 40 years' experience as a practicing physician, teacher, researcher, and leader of a large, urban, public healthcare system. About 10 years into my 20 years as CEO of the healthcare system, I became increasingly convinced that although we had new drugs and technologies, we were basically providing healthcare in the same way we did when I was an intern more than 40 years ago. When I shared this concern with my physician colleagues, one common response was: "We are doing things the same way because it must be the right way." All you had to do to know that wasn't true was to watch the activity in any clinic or on any hospital unit. No one would have consciously designed the work the way it was being done. Therefore, we began to look at how one could actually make healthcare work right. Was there some medicine out there that healthcare could take that could heal at least some of its current dysfunction? After a year of study, we concluded that Lean was the medicine that healthcare needed (Gabow et al., 2005).

Our seven-year Lean journey at Denver Health proved this to be correct. Lean was the medicine; the quality, financial, and employee engagement results were amazing.

The quality of care achieved was impressive, particularly given the vulnerability of the populations we served. Denver Health achieved an observed-to-expected mortality of almost 0.5, the lowest observed-to-expected mortality among the academic health center members of the University Healthsystem Consortium in 2011 (UHC).

The financial results were equally impressive. Denver Health realized almost $200 million of well-documented, hard financial benefit over seven years, $50 million in 2012.

Employees enthusiastically embraced Lean. Of Denver Health's employees, 83% affirmed that they understood how Lean helped us maintain our mission.

There are few, if any other, approaches that hit the target on quality, cost, and employee empowerment. In my decades in healthcare, I, as others in healthcare, tried many approaches to reducing cost and increasing quality. Lean was the most powerful approach to improvement and engagement I had ever seen.

From both a teacher's and a researcher's perspective, I believe that healthcare advances should be shared with others: documented, presented, and published. None of us should have to reinvent the wheel. There is too much to fix in healthcare to be reinventing. Hence, this book.

At its core it is simply a "How to" book on Lean implementation in a healthcare system: what you need to know and how to use what you know to achieve Lean transformation. This book's primary goal is to share Denver Health's Lean journey in order to encourage or facilitate that journey for other healthcare leaders who are searching for an approach to improve healthcare delivery.

This book does contain foundational information on Lean and many experiences and insights from others, but it is not intended to be a scholarly study of Toyota Production Systems (TPS) or Lean. We do discuss in detail Toyota/Lean philosophy, concepts, and tools as understanding them creates the necessary foundation for the actual "doing of Lean." Although we have tried to use commonly accepted definitions for these concepts and tools, the readers will find that, as in any discipline, some practitioners and scholars of Lean will have somewhat different usages.

The book is aimed at CEOs and senior leadership who must be at the head of the institution's Lean parade, as well as those who are facilitating the institution's Lean journey and those active Lean participants who want to learn more. Physicians and other clinical leaders should find the book useful as we have tried to tie the Lean principles, tools, exercises, and outcomes to how we have learned medicine and how we care for patients.

To add the richness of everyday examples and frontline experience to the perspective of a CEO and physician leader, I have a coauthor (Goodman) who oversaw the Lean Systems Improvement Department at Denver Health. (When "I" is used in the text, it refers to Dr. Gabow.)

Just as we learn patient care from real patients, this book contains examples from Denver Health's Lean journey. Also, as with caring for patients, we get better at Lean by doing it. Therefore, the book contains many exercises to help you get your feet wet in Lean. There is a temptation for busy people (CEOs, etc.) to skip the exercises, but we would strongly encourage every reader to take the extra minutes to do them. The exercises start you actually doing Lean, which begins your understanding of its simplicity and power.

We encourage you to read the entire book starting with Chapter 1 and ending with Chapter 9 at the outset of your Lean journey, just as you would read the entire MapQuest® route before you start to drive to avoid a wrong turn. However, a brief overview of the chapter's contents may direct you to areas of particular interest. The first four chapters incorporate information from the literature and the experience of others, as well as Denver Health's experience. The last five chapters deal primarily with Denver Health's Lean journey. The first chapter sets the stage for why healthcare needs healing. Chapter 2 focuses at a 30,000-foot level on the components of the Lean journey that require the focus and attention from the CEO and senior leadership. These are elaborated on in greater detail in Chapters 6 and 7. Chapters 3 and 4 provide a foundational understanding of the Lean principles, Toyota's key tenets, and the working concepts that were used by Simpler (Denver Health's Lean consultants) for implementation. Chapter 5 is a detailed description of the tools in the Lean tool box: what they are, how they are used, and examples of their application in healthcare. Chapters 6 and 7 lay out the structure and implementation that Denver Health utilized for its Lean journey. Chapters 8 and 9 detail the metrics used to assess our efforts and the outcomes from the Lean transformation. CEOs and other senior executives may want to read Chapter 9 and the milestones in our Lean journey (Table A.1) first to convince themselves of the value of Lean and give them an incentive to read the other eight chapters.

The relevant characteristics of Denver Health, detailed in Table I.1, will be useful in placing Denver Health's journey in an institutional context. It is worth noting that Denver Health is a safety net institution with a large amount of uncompensated care and limited discretionary resources. That environment did not limit Denver Health's ability to invest in the Lean effort. In fact, it created a reason to look for a different path. Therefore, institutions with the same or greater resources should not see resource allocation as a barrier to the Lean journey.

We believe Lean is the needed prescription, the powerful medicine, that can help heal our ailing healthcare system. We also believe you will feel the same joy from having Lean medicine make your institution better as you do from seeing your patients improve from the right care.

TABLE I.1

Characteristics of Denver Health

Type of institution: Independent, public, academic, urban, integrated safety net delivery system

Components: 500-bed acute care hospital, Level I trauma center; all eight Denver federally qualified health centers with primary care, dental care, pharmacy, Women, Infant, and Children (WIC) nutrition program; 15 school-based clinics; public health department for city/county; wholly owned HMO for commercial, Medicare, Medicaid, CHIP; 100-bed nonmedical detoxification center; 911 paramedic system for Denver; integrated call center with regional poison center, nurse advice line, occupational health line, appointment center, transfer center and translation center

Patient characteristics: 183,000 individual users, equivalent to one in three Denver residents. 70% ethnic minorities; 30% non-English speakers; 38% uninsured

Volumes: 25,000 inpatient admissions; 87,000 paramedic 911 calls; 115,000 emergency department and urgent care visits; 416,000 federally qualified health center (FQHC) patient visits; 64,000 WIC visits; 75,000 specialty clinic visits; 19,000 occupational health visits; 52,000 public health visits; 28,000 detoxification visits; 91,000 nurse advice line calls; 214,000 poison and drug center calls; 1,000,000 outpatient prescriptions

Financial information: $737,771,243 operating budget; $450 million uninsured care; approximately $27 million city/county uninsured care payment

Employment: 5,600 employees

Physician relationship: Employed physician model, 336 employed physicians. All physicians full-time academic appointments at University of Colorado School of Medicine. Shared graduate medical education program with the University of Colorado School of Medicine for most disciplines and three independent programs; 249 interns, residents, and fellows at any given time

---

Source: Data from 2012.

1

Why Worry about American Healthcare

You will hear some people say that America has the best healthcare system in the world, which would lead one to ask, "Why worry?" There is, in fact, a great deal to make all of us worry.

THOSE LEFT OUT

America may have the best healthcare system, if you are well insured with first-dollar coverage and if you can actually access that best healthcare when you need it. These remain big "ifs." Even given the historic passage of the Patient Protection and Affordable Care Act (known as the ACA) in 2010 that was intended to expand insurance coverage greatly, all the "ifs" are unlikely to be completely resolved by one congressional action.

In 2011, prior to the implementation of the ACA, approximately 50 million people in this country were uninsured (Kaiser Family Foundation, 2014). Moreover, the likelihood of an individual being uninsured substantially depends on that person's income, employment, ethnicity, and, surprisingly, where he or she lives. In 2012 the Commonwealth Fund's Commission on a High Performing Health System examined 306 local healthcare areas in the United States. That study found that among adults ages 18 to 64 years old some areas of Massachusetts had about 5% of this group uninsured, whereas some areas of Texas had more than 50% of this group uninsured (Commonwealth Fund Commission on a High Performing Health System, 2012). Given the Supreme Court's 2012 decision in *NFIB v. Sebelius* and the consequent states' flexibility in implementing the Medicaid expansion component of the ACA, this geographic disparity is likely to remain in the near future.

Individuals without health insurance have substantial barriers to accessing healthcare (Collins et al., 2013). Moreover, many individuals who are privately insured have high deductible insurance and copayments or substantial coinsurance when they do access care (Collins et al., 2013). These payment requirements can be a barrier to accessing care and to compliance with therapeutic interventions such as medication adherence and preventive care.

This lack of universal health insurance coverage and the gaps that occur even with insurance coverage have made illness a financial burden on many families and a major cause of bankruptcy for Americans. No other developed country has its population at such financial risk due to illness. It is difficult to understand how this lack of insurance, the barriers to healthcare access, and the range of disparities could fit with the idea that the American health system is the best in the world.

EXERCISE

Who is left out in your community? What are the health consequences to those individuals and to the health of your community? Go to the Commonwealth Foundation website (Commonwealthfund.org/publications/scorecards) and look at the national, state, and local scorecards for your state for details on access, cost, quality, and outcomes or the Robert Wood Johnson Foundation (countyhealthrankings.org) for County Health Rankings and Roadmaps, which details a number of the important social determinants of health and health outcomes.

HUGE COST

One might deduce that because 50 million people in America did not have healthcare prior to the ACA—a situation that does not occur in other developed countries—that American healthcare would be less costly than that of other developed nations. In fact, America spends twice as much per capita as do other developed countries (Commonwealth Fund Commission on a High Performing Health System, 2013). Over the last four decades the growth in healthcare costs exceeded the GDP rate of growth in 31 of the 40 years (IOM, 2013; Keehan, Sisko, and Truffer, 2011). Although the rate of increase in healthcare costs has slowed in the last several years, healthcare now consumes 18% of GDP (Commonwealth Fund

Commission on a High Performing Health System, 2013). America spends $2.8 trillion on healthcare. This makes American healthcare equal to the fifth largest GDP of the world's countries (World Bank, 2014). This enormous healthcare expenditure has many consequences:

1. Americans have growing concerns about the federal deficit that will burden future generations. Managing the deficit will require reducing total healthcare costs.
2. The healthcare expenditure limits America's ability to invest in other priorities such as education, infrastructure, the environment, and innovation.
3. This cost and its disparate resource consumption reduces America's competitiveness in the global marketplace.
4. The fact that we are spending $2.8 trillion dollars on healthcare means that many individuals and institutions are making large amounts of money from the current overly expensive system. This makes those individuals and institutions likely to oppose any change that reduces healthcare costs in their domains.
5. America is not getting the value it should from this burdensome expenditure. The Institute of Medicine has estimated that 30% to 40% of all the healthcare expenditures are waste, adding up to $765 billion per year (IOM, 2013). This does not add one jot to Americans' health and may, in fact, even worsen their health through inappropriate care. My experience as a CEO of a large health system and as a practitioner of Lean has convinced me that this is a substantial underestimate of the true waste.

EXERCISE

Go back to the Commonwealth Foundation website and review the international cost comparisons (Commonwealthfund.org). Also go to the Dartmouth Atlas (Dartmouthatlas.org) and look at the cost in your region compared to other regions.

QUALITY CHASM

Given our staggering healthcare costs, a critically thinking individual would likely conclude that the quality of American healthcare should be exceptional, exceeding that of the countries that spend half as much. However, the data lead to quite a different conclusion.

In 1999 the Institute of Medicine released a groundbreaking report, "To Err is Human: Building a Safer Health System" (IOM, 1999). This report shocked us by estimating that as many as 100,000 people die every year from hospital errors. Other reports present equally sobering data. A report from the Rand Corporation revealed that Americans only receive 50% of the care they should receive and some of the care that they do receive is either not indicated or even harmful (McGlynn et al., 2003; IOM, 2013).

A series of studies by the Commonwealth Fund over a number of years compares the outcomes of American healthcare to that of other developed countries. In a recent report assessing 42 variables of healthcare, we earn a grade of 64 out of 100 (Commonwealth Fund Commission on a High Performing Health System, 2011). Moreover, just as there is substantial variation in the uninsured rates across states, there is great variation among states and even within the same state for these quality indicators (Commonwealth Fund Commission on a High Performing Health System, 2011). Variation in quality is also seen across racial and socioeconomic groups.

EXERCISE

Go back to the Commonwealth Foundation website (Commonwealthfund. org) and look again at the national and state scorecards and the Robert Wood Johnson Foundation County Health Rankings and Roadmap (countyhealthrankings.org).

PREVAILING CULTURE OF HEALTHCARE

American healthcare is delivered via siloed, fragmented, and largely uncoordinated delivery models and is funded by multiple and often misaligned payment models. These factors lead to duplication; multiple and occasionally conflicting regulations; burdens for patients, providers, and payers; and waste. The move toward integrated systems, accountable care organizations (ACOs), and bundled/global payment models may begin to address these issues. Moreover, in any given American healthcare institution, there are hierarchical administrative and decision-making structures and silos that arise from the increasing specialization of every professional discipline. These silos create multiple handoffs, waits, duplication, and, of course, waste. The emerging efforts for team care and coordination of care transitions may lessen some aspects of these problems.

EXERCISE

In your institution can you name some silos that reduce efficiency and quality? Think about examples such as overlaps or handoffs that may occur between human resource and payroll, or separation of inpatient and out-patient services. In your institution are there inefficiencies because groups are not working at the top of their licenses because of discipline silos? Think about examples such as CRNAs, psychologists, social workers, PAs, and NPs.

IMPACT ON THE REST OF THE WORLD

This book is focused on American healthcare, however, healthcare issues do not end at our borders. The most obvious and direct impact of American healthcare's dysfunction on others is that as healthcare gobbles up more of our resources, less is available to aid developing countries not only with healthcare, but also with a range of other critical investments.

Other developed countries are also seeing their healthcare costs rise, contributing to their own economic problems. They, too, would like solutions that would lower costs and improve quality. Therefore, just as we have exported aspects of our dysfunctional system, we could now export solutions. In fact, a number of both developed and developing countries are beginning to use Lean as an approach to both improving and creating healthcare systems.

POTENTIAL SOLUTIONS

We need to face the reality that America doesn't have the best healthcare system in the world. We need to worry about the people who suffer because they don't have health insurance or access to care; we need to worry about the unsustainable and crippling costs; we need to worry about the quality and value of care we are getting. But worry without solutions, or concern without action will be useless.

Both the state and federal governments are taking a wide array of steps to address the issues of coverage, cost, quality, and care coordination. Some important changes emanating from both the ACA and states' efforts are near-universal insurance coverage (depending on states embracing Medicaid expansion), more integrated systems of care, greater care coordination, broader use of health information technology, more patient engagement, movement away from fee for service payments, assessment and dissemination of evidence-based care, and greater quality and price transparency.

Although these are important actions by federal and state governments, the fruits of these policy changes will only occur if individual healthcare systems are transformed. These transformations will require leadership that is committed to change and will require clear methods to achieve meaningful transformation (IOM, 2013). We need to identify, prescribe, and administer some powerful medicine to our ailing healthcare system. Lean can provide a disciplined structured approach to lowering costs, improving quality, and enlisting the entire healthcare workforce in transformation and in meaningfully engaging patients. Lean may just be the medicine we need.

2

Role of Leadership in Health System Transformation

There are many thoughtful treatises on transformational leadership. Although leadership is not the central theme of this book, omitting a discussion of the role of the leaders could result in some believing that Lean transformation can occur in the absence of active leadership, commitment, and engagement, which is the antithesis of the truth. Leadership is essential because transformation is not tweaking. Transformation is radical change in what the health system believes, what it values, and what it does. It is not becoming a bigger caterpillar—it is becoming a butterfly.

There are at least three key roles for leadership in healthcare system transformation:

1. Defining the journey
2. Implementing the journey
3. Committing to outcome

DEFINING THE JOURNEY

Perhaps the most important role of a leader in transformation is to create the vision. The vision should be noble, important, and a stretch to achieve.

Example

Denver Health's vision for its journey was to create a mature culture committed to reducing waste in order to perfect the patient's experience and become a model for the nation.

At first blush, this may seem arrogant in the context of a public safety net institution that serves the poor and vulnerable. On the other hand, such a goal conveyed to the employees that the institution's leaders believed they had the capacity to achieve something worthy of their effort and commitment. This is in line with the vision that Toyota had at the beginning of its journey to become a globally responsible world leader in automobile manufacturing. Similarly, a past CEO of Toyota voiced an amazing goal in the context of that vision: "We must design a car that can cross the whole world with a single tank of gas, that will clean the air as it operates and that will never harm a single pedestrian" (Koenigsaecker, 2013). Given this vision and goal, our goal seems much less audacious and eminently achievable.

EXERCISE

Has your organization developed, articulated, and disseminated a vision for your journey? If you have, is it noble? Is it important? Is it a stretch? If you haven't developed such a vision statement, doing so should be a first step.

A clear and noble vision must be linked to a defined path to achieve the vision or it is simply another empty slogan or institutional tagline. The path Denver Health chose to achieve its vision emerged from a year of study supported by the Agency for Healthcare Research and Quality, involved multiple components, and is detailed in an AHRQ "Toolkit" (Gabow et al., 2005). Some key components of this effort to define the path were:

> Formation of an external advisory group, mostly not from healthcare
> Telephone consultations and site visits
> Employee focus groups
> Patient focus groups
> Process mapping

The advisory group provided diverse perspectives on organizational change. This along with site visits to nonhealthcare corporations such as FedEx and Dell and some healthcare organizations that had experienced transformational efforts informed our transformation path.

As CEO, I conducted multiple focus groups with employees, beginning with housekeepers. The grouping of individuals by job class instead of using open forums created an environment in which individuals felt comfortable engaging in discussion. Employees were asked to respond to two key questions:

> "What do you see happening to patients which you don't think should happen?"
>
> "What keeps you from working efficiently?"

These meetings served to inform the employees that transformational efforts were beginning and underscored their role in this effort, putting into practice Lean's respect for people.

EXERCISE

Preferably the CEO or another senior leader should conduct several employee focus groups asking these two questions. After you have done a few such groups, you may decide to conduct these throughout your organization.

Patient focus groups were conducted with insured and uninsured patients and with English- and Spanish-speaking patients to reflect the individuals whom we served. The questions revolved around the core of the patient's experience, focusing on how patients and their families wished to be engaged in their care and how they wished to access information. This put into practice the Lean principle that "the customer defines value." The voice of the customer is an important Lean concept we discuss in more detail in Chapter 4. This concept aligns with healthcare's emerging emphasis on meaningful patient engagement.

EXERCISE

Therefore, consider conducting at least one patient focus group that is representative of the individuals whom you serve in order to begin to gain this perspective.

Process mapping is discussed in greater detail in Chapter 5 as a key Lean tool. However, we ventured into it at this juncture not as a Lean tool, but as a way to convince ourselves that we really had waste and needed change. The process mapping exercise is not for the squeamish. An industrial engineer who had never been in healthcare was hired to map a range of processes from the food service tray line, to a nurse's activities over a shift, to residents' workdays. All the data that emerged from these observations led to a single response: "Please tell me this is not what we do!" Yet, these detailed observations reflected what we did do, not just at Denver Health, but also, almost assuredly, throughout American healthcare. For more details on these observations, the reader is referred to the "Toolkit" (Gabow et al., 2005).

EXERCISE

If you think your organization is already "Lean" (as almost everyone does at the start of the journey) and are unconvinced that the processes in your institution are dysfunctional and wasteful, hire an industrial engineer or ask an employee with this skill to map a few processes. Two informative employee groups to map are a floor nurse's and house officer's day (if you have house staff) and a good process to map is the discharge process.

Our current healthcare processes evolved, not with genetic precision of survival of the fittest, but rather more randomly through "make do," "get it done," and "workaround" responses to our siloed and uncoordinated care. Very few, if any, current healthcare processes grew out of structured observations and careful planning. Most processes emerged to meet the provider's and institution's needs (not usually the patient's needs or convenience), to comply with regulations, or to deal with institutional physical layouts that were the result of expansions that occurred over many years.

At the end of this year of assessment, we concluded that whole system transformation would require focus on a set of six (initially there were only five; right service was added later) tightly linked efforts centered on the patient and his or her family. These were: right process, right service, right environment, right people, right communication, and right reward. The total effort was dubbed "Getting It Right (who wants to get it wrong): Perfecting the Patient Experience" and the visual was a multipiece puzzle with the centerpiece being the patient and the family. This concept of "Getting It Right" relates directly to Toyota's views: "Do what is right and do it the right way" (Hino, 2002).

We focused our attention on the "Right Process" for which we chose Lean as the path to achieve that goal. Ultimately, Lean became an approach for the rest of the components. However, at the beginning of our journey we did not understand the broad power of Lean.

EXERCISE

Define the components of your transformation journey. In keeping with the Lean concept of visual management create a picture of the components of your journey to excellence and disseminate it.

IMPLEMENTING THE JOURNEY

Successful journeys need to follow the path they have chosen. To facilitate that, the road should be clear, well-marked, and maintained. This requires structure and discipline. If you want others in your organization to be on this journey with you, you need to teach the path both by imparting knowledge and by walking the path yourself and by having all the leadership team walking the path. The details of our Lean management structure and deployment are detailed in Chapters 6 and 7.

COMMITTING TO OUTCOME

We can only know we have made the journey we intended if we have a defined destination. You need to establish and track metrics to let you know that you have arrived or at least that you are still on the right road. Moreover, metrics are only useful if feedback on performance is provided to those who are engaged in the effort. The visual management component of Lean provides true transparency. We know that knowledge is power and organizational transparency distributes that power to everyone. The details of the metrics, the feedback loops, transparency, and outcomes of our Lean journey are detailed in Chapters 8 and 9.

3

Why Pick Lean for Healthcare Transformation

We chose Lean as the path for our healthcare system's transformation because it is a:

Noble Philosophy
Robust Tool Set
Easy to Learn Approach
Enabler of Cultural Transformation

PHILOSOPHY OF LEAN

Lean evolved from the Japanese Toyota automobile manufacturing company. It is disappointing that it didn't come from healthcare, because its core philosophy reflects what should be the core philosophy of healthcare. Lean is built on two pillars: respect for people and continuous improvement (Koenigsaecker, 2013).

Are there any concepts more core to healthcare than these? As we proceed through this book, we show that Lean's respect for people truly empowers the workforce to use their talents and knowledge to perfect every process. Rapid improvement events (RIEs) are week-long employee events focused on a given process and are described in detail in Chapters 5 and 7. These RIEs turn hierarchy on its head. The concept of letting anyone "stop the line" if they see a problem reflects amazing trust in each person to have the information he or she needs to do the job and to use that knowledge correctly. The Lean commitment to ubiquitous production boards is a powerful commitment to transparency, demonstrating that everyone can and should have access to relevant information. In my 40 years in healthcare, Lean is the only approach I have seen that truly empowers everyone and converts empowerment from a meaningless catchphrase to an operational reality.

A central focus of Lean is to identify and eliminate waste. This focus on waste can be applied to an existing process or to the development of a new process. From a Lean perspective, waste is a process or a component of a process that uses resources but adds no value to the customer, something the customer wouldn't want to pay for if he had the choice. There are components of a process that are value-added steps and non-value-added steps or waste. Of course, we want to keep the value-added steps and eliminate the non-value-added steps. We should ask ourselves, "Why would we want to keep steps in any process that add no value?" It is hard to come up with a logical answer. A wonderful aspect of eliminating non-value-added steps is that it does not require any additional resources (Cooper, 2011). There is a small catch: not all non-value-added steps can be eliminated. There are non-value-added steps/waste that a customer would likely not want to pay for but are a necessary component of the current healthcare environment. Even considering that some waste must stay, there is a great deal that can and should be eliminated. How much waste do you think there is in processes untouched by Lean? Some experts say 95% (Koenigsaecker, 2013; Joint Commission Resources, 2008). Initially, we thought this estimate was absurd. However, Lean taught us to see waste and made us believe that 60% to 90% of every untouched healthcare process is waste.

EXERCISE

Think about your own last visit to a doctor or a healthcare facility. Write down what part of that process you would be willing to pay for if you had a choice. What percentage of the visit time was of direct value to you? Let us give you some ideas. Did you have to wait on a call to make an appointment? When you arrived for the appointment, did the clerk ask you questions that should have been available to him or her on an electronic record? Did you have to wait in the waiting room? When you were taken into the exam room, did you have to wait for the doctor? Did the doctor ask you questions about information that was in your record? At the end of the visit with the doctor, did you have to wait for another step? Did you have to go somewhere else for blood tests or a radiology study? Add up the time of these wastes and see what percentage of the total visit time was of value to you.

EIGHT WASTES

Lean has identified the eight key wastes shown in Table 3.1 (Toyota and some experts use seven) (Koenigsaecker, 2013; Liker, 2004). Obviously, these wastes have clear examples in manufacturing. Interestingly, one can also quickly identify many examples of these wastes in healthcare (Joint Commission Resources, 2008). This suggests that any human activity can easily fall into ways of doing things that lead to waste. The list below should get you thinking about some wastes that have become accepted as a part of healthcare. Clearly, some items could be put into more than one category, but the identification of waste is more important than a specific category. If this list, which is only a tip of the waste iceberg, does not convince you that we are mired in waste, nothing will.

1. Overproduction:
   a. Manufacturing example: Producing a product that has not yet been requested or needed.
   b. Healthcare examples: Patient remaining in hospital past medical necessity. Pharmacy filling prescriptions that the patient never picks up. Ordering laboratory tests "just in case" or radiology exams that are duplicative or unnecessary.
2. Waiting: This is one of the most ubiquitous wastes in healthcare. It is noteworthy that often a healthcare organization's response to waiting is to add "amenities:" flat screen televisions, magazines, telephones, Wi-Fi access, and coffee carts. We have focused resources on

TABLE 3.1

The Eight Wastes
Overproduction
Waiting
Unnecessary Transport
Overprocessing
Excess Inventory
Unnecessary Movement
Defects
Unused/Misused Human Talent

Source: J. Liker, *The Toyota Way*, 2004, New York: McGraw-Hill, pp.28–29.

making the waiting more pleasant rather than focusing on eliminating the waste of waiting.

   a. Manufacturing example: Employees waiting for work to come to them because the previous process work was being "batched."

   b. Healthcare examples: Patients sitting in "waiting rooms." The mere fact that we have waiting rooms everywhere in healthcare demonstrates a key problem with flow and an overall acceptance of this waste. Patients being "boarded" in an emergency department waiting for a bed. Patients staying in the hospital waiting for a procedure not available on weekends. Patients waiting for discharge until doctors finish rounds and write orders. Physicians waiting for patients. There are many examples of this including surgeons waiting for patients in the operating room because some preoperative process failed or simply that the room turnover was delayed by roadblocks in that process. Doctors waiting for patients to be checked in at a registration desk. Often this occurs because there is no visual management so the clerks don't know the doctor is waiting and the doctor doesn't know patients are there. Providers waiting for information or results.

3. Unnecessary transport: This refers to conveyance or moving inventory from one place to another.

   a. Manufacturing example: Moving materials long distances because of inefficient plant design.

   b. Healthcare examples: Having all supplies come to a central loading dock and then being moved around the institution. Moving patients due to availability of patient rooms with "male" or "female" beds. Moving a cancer patient from one area of the hospital or clinic to another area for treatments or tests needed in the same visit.

4. Overprocessing:

   a. Manufacturing example: Letting paint dry on a vehicle for 14 hours when only 10 are needed.

   b. Healthcare examples: Numerous staff asking the patient the same questions. Numerous forms with similar information. Printing hard copies of data in the electronic record. Multiple copies of items in information system. Many cc's on e-mails. Multiple people doing the same task. Different discipline teams (nurses and physicians) doing separate rounds. Interns and residents "prerounding" before attending rounds. Patient requiring face-to-face visit to obtain laboratory or radiology results. Administering IV antibiotics when oral drugs are appropriate. Performing an unneeded test such as MRI for back pain. Unnecessary C-sections.

5. Excess inventory: This waste is often viewed by manufacturing as the most critical waste in terms of the dollars it ties up. In manufacturing, inventory waste is often expressed as "Work in Progress" (WIP) referring to a product waiting to be worked on at any point in the process. If I can only work on one widget at a time, then having a batch of 12 widgets would represent excess inventory. Then, of course, there is the more usual understanding of inventory. We often think of inventory only as goods, but as Liker (2004) points out we also need to think about "information inventory," when information is produced before it is used. This is particularly relevant to healthcare in the current health information technology age.

    a. Manufacturing example: Ordering parts and supplies in excess of need and storing them.

    b. Healthcare examples: As distasteful as it may be to refer to human beings as "inventory waiting to be worked on," a waiting room full of patients is the healthcare analogy of inventory waiting to be worked. ICU data systems generate hundreds of pages of data including reams of vital signs or monitor readings that remain unchanged hour after hour. Cardiology or radiology having on hand more stents than are needed, often becoming outdated. Low inventory turns in pharmacy. Building unnecessary hospital beds. Unnecessary trauma centers in a region.

6. Unnecessary movement: This is waste associated with hunting and gathering for supplies or even excessive reaching.

    a. Manufacturing example: An employee having to get up and walk to a different area for a tool.

    b. Healthcare examples: Physicians having patients in multiple hospital units requiring teams to spend substantial time walking. Poorly laid out operating rooms with nurses walking around the department or room for equipment. Nurses walking from a patient's room to a central supply area for routinely needed care items.

7. Defects: In healthcare this is the most important waste as it can truly harm the patient, creating both morbidity and mortality. Defects also create enormous amounts of wasteful rework to fix the problem.
   a. Manufacturing example: Defective part that causes the product to fail.
   b. Healthcare example: Registration omissions or errors. Billing errors. Illegible handwriting. Mislabeled patient specimen. Utilizing wrong diagnostic test. Making the incorrect diagnosis. Hospital-acquired infection. Giving the patient the wrong drug. Performing wrong site surgery.
8. Unused or misused human talent:
   a. Manufacturing example: Not allowing employees to stop the line when they see a defect.
   b. Healthcare examples: Having an intern or resident call for appointments for the patient. Not letting employees work to the level of their training and license. Having a professional perform a task that could be done by a nonprofessional worker or having a more highly trained and more expensive professional perform a task that could be performed well by a professional with less extensive training. Not empowering a nurse to stop an OR procedure when an inadequate timeout occurred.

EXERCISE

Write this list of wastes from Table 3.1 on a piece of paper and put it on a clipboard. Go out to any area where work is done in your institution (it can be absolutely any work area). Stand there for 30 minutes and write all the wastes you see using this list; it will be long. You should have something in every category of waste. Someone who is using the Lean lens could get over 50 examples in 30 minutes.

This zeal to remove waste is not an afterthought of Lean; it is deeply embedded in the Toyota philosophy. Toyota leaders are said to have linked respect and waste in this way (Simpler Sensei):

"Waste is disrespectful to humanity because it squanders scarce resources."
"Waste is disrespectful to workers because it asks them to do work with no value."

The elimination of waste is not simply respect for humanity and for the workforce. For those of us in healthcare, it is also about respect for our patients. Thus, we have added:

> Waste is disrespectful to the patient because it asks her to endure processes of no value.

Given the realization of the excessive cost of American healthcare, we have also added:

> Waste is disrespectful to the citizens by asking them to pay taxes for work with no value.

Elimination of waste and the consequent improvement of processes have three very clear effects in healthcare:

1. It saves money.
2. It saves lives.
3. It saves jobs.

The tight linkage that Lean creates between lower cost and higher quality fits perfectly with the growing emphasis on delivering high-value healthcare.

4

Toyota Principles and Working Concepts of Lean

14 TOYOTA PRINCIPLES

Toyota articulated 14 principles that clearly relate to the philosophy of respect for people, continuous improvement, and the elimination of waste (Liker, 2004). These principles are worth listing as they provide underpinnings to "the doing" of Lean. We have added comments after these principles to begin your thinking about their relationship and applicability to healthcare. As you read the book, the translation of principles into working concepts, tools, and examples will give more robust meaning to this list.

1. "Base your management decisions on a long-term philosophy, even at the expense of short-term financial goals."

   This first requires that every healthcare institution actually have a clear long-term philosophy. Every healthcare institution has concerns about short-term financial goals. This may have greater emphasis in the for-profit sector in which quarterly earnings are important. However, this concern about short-term financial goals does not make this principle impossible to achieve, given that Toyota also lives in the world of quarterly earnings. This principle would ask us to go beyond short-term earnings in designing institutional goals.

2. "Create continuous process flow to bring problems to the surface."

   We rarely have mapped the flow of our healthcare processes, let alone design them to flow smoothly. Therefore, the barriers that patients experience have been hidden for decades.

3. "Use pull systems to avoid overproduction."

   For healthcare, as for Toyota, this can apply to just-in-time services and inventory. In healthcare there are other implications. For example, adding beds in an area without demonstrating clear geographic demand has been shown to correlate with increased hospital admissions (a type of overproduction). A similar human resource example is adding more specialists in a geographic area than are needed for optimal patient care, which again has been demonstrated to increase specialty use. Both of these are about pushing use rather than pulling care based on patient needs.

4. "Level out the workload."

   We rarely use the data we have on variation in workload to schedule procedures and employees' work times. We schedule our workers' time by established shifts and hours of operation. We often schedule work such as surgeries for the convenience of the providers.

5. "Build a culture of stopping to fix problems, to get it (quality) right the first time."

   It has not been our culture to stop a process to get the quality right; therefore, we have not developed systems to accomplish this goal. Timeouts before procedures are one example of healthcare embracing this concept. If it were a ubiquitous part of our culture, we would need fewer mortality and morbidity conferences.

6. "Standardized tasks are the foundation for continuous improvement and employee empowerment."

   Variability is common in any healthcare process both within one institution and certainly between institutions. This often leads to overuse, errors, and waste.

7. "Use visual controls so no problems are hidden."

   Walk through any healthcare system and you will rarely see visual controls that are being utilized to maximize flow and show the problems to the workers in real time.

8. "Use only reliable, thoroughly tested technology that serves your people and processes."

   We often adopt new and expensive technology without clear evidence of the benefit of its use, without knowledge of its potential harm, and without clear cost–benefit information. Often an institution adds the newest technology to be the first on the block with something new.

9. "Grow leaders, who thoroughly understand the work, live the philosophy, and teach it to others."

Principles 9, 10, and 12 are closely linked concepts. Often in healthcare leaders are office-based individuals whose understanding of the work is based on what they hear from others rather than seeing for themselves (Principle 12). As leaders engage in mapping, oversee value streams, participate in rapid improvement events, and round from production boards, they truly understand the work and this then cascades to those who report to them. The leaders model the desired behaviors and become coaches.

10. "Develop exceptional people and teams who follow your company's philosophy."

     Often in our institutions we have not had a either "True North"—a clear goal—or clear alignment and cascading of goals from the top to the very front lines. Lean offers a way to achieve this. The Toyota principle of respect for people and its outgrowth of turning every worker into a problem solver help to operationalize this principle.

11. "Respect your expanded network of partners and suppliers by challenging them and helping them improve."

     We have often relegated our suppliers to vendors and thus we often have failed to engage them in reducing waste and adding value. Toyota shows us how this can all be integrated into one flow.

12. "Go and see for yourself to thoroughly understand the situation."

     As discussed in Principle 9, there is no substitute for going to where the work is done. As leaders, this has not been our modus operandi. Once you have done it, you will see it is how you find truth.

13. "Make decisions slowly by consensus, thoroughly considering all options; implement decisions rapidly."

     In healthcare, we often make decisions via large committees with numerous stakeholders. Decisions often do take a long time but they do not often use the disciplined approach that Toyota has developed to assess all options and aligning them with True North. The possibility of many points of veto often prevents rapid implementation of the chosen path in our institutions. (Think about many change orders!)

14. "Become a learning organization through relentless reflection and continuous improvement."

     This construct is beginning to enter the healthcare vocabulary and thinking in part through the efforts of the Institute of Medicine Round Table on Science and Value Driven Healthcare.

WORKING CONCEPTS OF LEAN

One of the powerful aspects of Lean is that the philosophy and principles come to life in working concepts and tools. Several teachers of Lean have condensed these 14 principles into a smaller set of working concepts (Liker, 2004; Simpler Business System®). We have chosen five of these that we have found most useful:

1. Customer defines value (Simpler Business System).
2. Standardize to solve and improve (Simpler Business System).
3. Deliver value on demand without waste (Simpler Business System)/ Flow the process (Liker, 2004).
4. Manage for daily improvement (Simpler Business System)/Relentless pursuit of perfection (Liker, 2004).
5. Mutual respect and shared responsibility enable higher performance (Simpler Business System).

Customer Defines Value

A foundational working concept of Lean is that the customer defines value, an obvious derivative of respect for people. Until quite recently this would have been a revolutionary idea for healthcare. It is a much more robust concept than the concept of patient satisfaction that has entered into our current healthcare vocabulary and thinking. Our systems have grown up largely to meet the needs of providers, institutions, and regulators, not the needs of the patient who is our most important customer. Some in healthcare, particularly providers, object to calling the patient a customer, as it seems to place the patients on the same level of someone going to Target to buy a wastebasket. We share that discomfort. Our patients are our partners in their care, not simply recipients of a service. That service is often of enormous consequence to them and their families, far beyond that experienced by the traditional customer. Nonetheless, the point of using the term *customer* is to underscore that we need to see the world from their perspective and understand that perspective. This Lean concept is in complete alignment with the growing emphasis on patient engagement and shared decision making. Surprisingly, when patients are engaged in shared decision making they often wish less-invasive and fewer low-yield procedures. Providers can be quite mistaken about what the patient defines as value when they do not listen to the voices of the patients or have a structured way to hear that voice.

This focus on the patient's voice and patient engagement is not to say that the providers' needs have no relevance. In fact, healthcare providers have many internal and external customers: pharmacy and central supply have nursing as an internal customer, consultants have primary care doctors as an internal customer, and registration clerks have the billing department as an internal customer. There are many such examples. These internal customers are important and often meeting their definition of value helps meet the value definition of the patient. Although these internal customers are quite relevant, they are not primary: the patient is at the center.

The external customers also have relevance. These customers include the regulatory and accrediting bodies and the payers. The latter are particularly important because unlike other commercial endeavors, the payer is not the direct recipient of the service, nor are they generally a partner in the care process (although some payers are becoming more active partners). Toyota has emphasized the external relationship with their vendors, teaching them, and linking them to their own process, underscoring the relevance of these groups to delivering value to their primary customer.

Exercise

Go to an area where work is done and look carefully to see if the work being done has been designed from the patient's perspective or the employees' perspectives. Ask yourself, "Would the patient see the process as ideal and the best use of his time, effort, and money?" You might even do something as simple as look at your cafeteria hours; do those hours meet the needs of the employees and patients' families?

Standardize to Solve and Improve

Standard work means that the work must be done in a specific way by every person, every time. But it goes beyond that: the standard work for every process should be the currently best-known, least wasteful way of performing the work and it must be done that way until a better way is found (Hino, 2002; Simpler Business System).

When we first were exposed to the idea of standard work and the Lean zeal to standardize every recurring process, it seemed at odds with the Lean pillar of continuous improvement: how could something always be the same and change at the same time? Was this an Eastern philosophical understanding of work? We came to understand that if the same activity were done differently and randomly by everyone, one could never see what was wrong. It is hard to see patterns in chaos unless you are a chaos theorist and there aren't many of those in healthcare.

Henry Ford, from whom Toyota actually learned much, stated "Today's standardization … is the necessary foundation on which tomorrow's improvement will be based" (Liker, 2004). Interestingly, the role of standardization can also be flipped the other way around, as was done by Toyota. "Invention becomes innovation only when stable duplication is achieved on a meaningful scale" (Hino, 2002).

The other critical outcome of standardization is quality. As Liker noted, " … you cannot guarantee quality without standard procedures for ensuring consistency in the process" (Liker, 2004).

The lack of standardization is ubiquitous in healthcare. In some ways this lack of standardization in healthcare emanates from the historic autonomy of the medical profession and the cottage industry nature of much of American healthcare. A craftperson or artisan's approach to care steers away from standardization; everyone is creating her own work of art (Cooper, 2011).

At the end of every rapid improvement event, the teams provide insights from the event and the most common, almost universal, observation is that the process lacked standard work or if standard work was ever created, it is not being followed by everyone, every time. Hand hygiene quickly comes to mind.

There are two interesting twists to the definition of standard work. On one hand, it is not some arbitrary way of working: it should be the least wasteful way. You certainly don't want to develop standard work that has non-value-added steps! The other twist is it should be the currently best-known way; it is not necessarily, or even likely, the ultimately best possible way.

EXERCISE

Have your executives or managers observe the performance of a single process in their area by eight or ten different people and see how often they all follow the same standard procedure. Have them take a look at the agendas and minutes of the committees that report to them. Are they standardized to deliver the information in the best-known way? Have your CMO look at initial orders for one condition from four or five different providers (assuming you don't have computerized physician order entry [CPOE] with order sets) and see how often they reflect one standard approach to care.

Often in clinical medicine, there is not clear indisputable evidence of the best therapeutic approach. Even in these settings, standardizing the process to a reasonable approach has great quality and financial benefits.

Example

Deep venous thrombosis (DVT or blood clots in the leg) and its sequelae, pulmonary thromboembolism, are major complications and causes of death of hospitalized patients (Michota, 2007). Often the disciplines of medicine, surgery, orthopedics, and obstetrics have differing views on the best approach and often individual practitioners within a discipline or within one hospital service take different approaches. Even more amazing, the same practitioner may have different practices at different times for similar clinical situations; so much for standardization! Denver Health's performance on the quality measure of the incidence of postoperative DVT was not good. Early in our Lean journey we asked ourselves if we could use the Lean rapid improvement event (RIE) approach to define standard work (more information and examples of RIEs are found in Chapter 7).

Eight individuals including five physicians became the team for this RIE. In four days they developed a common approach to postoperative anti-coagulation. The incidence of DVT markedly decreased as shown in Figure 4.1 (Data from the University Healthsystem Consortium UHC 2007–2012). Although some decrease in the rate had occurred from 2007 to 2008, Denver Health's rate was substantially above the expected rate given by the Agency

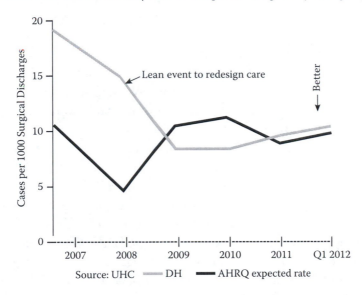

FIGURE 4.1
Impact of a rapid improvement event on postoperative venous thromboembolism. (From UHC Clinical Data Base/Resource Manager™. With permission fom UHC. All rights reserved.)

for Healthcare Research and Quality (AHRQ). After the RIE the rate fell and remained at or slightly above the AHRQ rate. In addition to the improvement in this quality measure, the standardization resulted in a more appropriate choice of therapy, saving $15,000/month by lessening the use of the most expensive, but often not indicated, anticoagulant (Biffl et al., 2011).

Deliver Value on Demand without Waste/Flow the Process

A principal outcome of elimination waste in a process is that the entire process flows smoothly without unwanted, wasteful stopping points. Delivering value on demand without waste integrates four Lean concepts:

1. Tight connections, having each step tightly linked to the step before and the step after
2. One-piece flow, which means exactly what it says, flowing one item through the whole process without having the item wait in a batch somewhere along the way
3. Pull (as opposed to push), having the process flow initiated by customer demand and not by some predicted need (push)
4. Standard work to enable the performance of the first three

Together these efforts create clean handoffs, eliminate batching, and allow a process to flow without waste only when the customer wants it or needs it every time.

The idea of one-piece flow deserves some special attention. Somewhere in our genome, perhaps when we moved from our hunting and gathering stage, we all acquired a love for batching (Womack and Jones, 2003). It makes so much sense intuitively: do a lot of the same work and create a stack of work so the next person will have a nice neat pile of work to do. A wonderful example of how really embedded batching is in our thinking is detailed in *Lean Thinking* (Womack and Jones, 2003). One of the authors asked his six- and nine-year-old daughters, "What is the best way to fold, address, seal, stamp, and mail the monthly issue of their mother's newsletter?" They emphatically told him, "Daddy, you should first fold them all, then put the address labels on all of them, etc." (Womack and Jones, 2003). Toyota turned this idea on its head with the concept of one-piece flow.

Let's do a little test to see if the two little girls or Toyota is right.

EXERCISE

At your next executive team meeting or your next meeting of your physician, nursing, or administrative leadership groups demonstrate the power of one-piece flow with this exercise (personal communication Gerald Harris, Simpler sensei).

First run: Start with 10 regular different colored markers and explain to the group that the markers represent people coming into the emergency department who need to be taken care of quickly and correctly. Explain that taking off the cap of each marker and replacing the cap represents taking care of one patient. Each person must remove and replace all 10 caps on the markers before passing to the person downstream. If there are any marks from the markers on people's hands, it's considered a defect. If a marker falls on the floor, it's a defect. Having the wrong colored cap on a marker is a defect. Assign a person to time the overall process and begin the first run. At the end of the first run record the total time it took for the markers to go from the first person to be finished by the last person. Record and add up all defects.

Second run: Inform the group they will still need to remove and replace the marker caps but now one at a time rather than doing all 10 before passing it on to the next person down the line. This is timed and the same rules for defects apply.

Final run: The participants will do the same as in the second run but now a participant cannot pass a marker to the next person until they receive a pull signal from the person downstream. That signal would be an open hand meaning the downstream person is ready to receive the marker from the person upstream. This is also timed and the same rules for defects apply.

The big surprise to most of us is that one-piece flow always wins and the third run is the best. In part, this is due to the fact that with batching there is always some work waiting for someone to act on it, adding time to the process.

In healthcare it is hard, but not impossible, to find examples of delivering value on demand without waste from the patient's perspective, examples of real pull. It is worth noting that the first four of these five examples relate to serious life-threatening emergencies:

1. Well-executed triage at a mass casualty event
2. Trauma response in a practiced Level I trauma center
3. Cardiopulmonary resuscitation performed by a designated high-functioning Cor Zero team
4. Door to balloon for cardiac patients
5. Patient-controlled anesthesia pumps

These first four are great examples of standard work, tight connections, one-piece flow, and pull. Everyone on the teams knows what he is to do (standard work), the handoffs are well defined and the next step happens when the preceding step is completed (tight connections), and it is clear that the patient event started the process flow (pull). The fourth example is particularly interesting because it often is publicly reported and perhaps transparency helps to put focus on delivering value on demand without waste for this process.

It seems that we can deliver value on demand without waste with structure, practice, and discipline in circumstances when we know effective flow means patient survival. This suggests that either we don't see the urgency or value in delivering value on demand without waste in more routine processes or that routine healthcare processes are so complicated that we rarely can see the flow in the same clear way that we can see the flow in a triggered and compressed event such as a cardiac arrest. I believe it is not that we don't see the value in flowing the process, but rather that we don't see the flow of more routine processes. Because we can't see the flow we are unaware of the barriers to the process flow. This is one reason why mapping the processes is so important.

The fifth example of delivering value on demand without waste is quite different. It is the use of patient-controlled anesthesia (PCA) pumps. Prior to the use of PCA pumps, postoperative patients either got pain medication at a set time, which may not have related to their pain cycle (push), or they had to ring a nurse call button whose response was frequently delayed (pull without response). The use of the PCA pump allows the patient to pull anesthesia when he or she is ready and get an immediate response.

One of the goals of using Lean in healthcare should be to enable the majority of our processes to deliver value on demand without waste.

EXERCISE

Can you describe a healthcare process you or a family member experienced recently? Did it deliver value on demand without any barriers? Do you think the providers were aware of the barriers to the process flow?

Manage for Daily Improvement and Relentlessly Pursue Perfection

Managing for daily improvement and relentless pursuit of perfection are linked concepts. In a way, managing for daily improvement represents a short-term horizon and the relentless pursuit of perfection represents a long-term horizon of excellence. The Lean Black Belts who were our cadre of Lean-trained leaders and who were distributed throughout Denver Health were the force that pushed the performance up a little bit every day by using Lean tools to see and eliminate the small wastes. In some ways the value streams (areas of focus) and the RIEs take aim at the larger issues and the longer term horizon. We all know that perfection is elusive, but chasing it is not a quixotic adventure; the chase keeps moving us closer to the healthcare that we need for everyone.

For daily improvement, visual management is critical. The team needs to know in real time how they are doing in comparison to the target state. Hiding performance (usually unconsciously) can only lead to poor performance.

EXERCISE

Can you describe a standard approach that your organization now uses for managing for daily improvement and for the relentless pursuit of perfection?

Mutual Respect and Shared Responsibility Enable Higher Levels of Performance

This concept emanates from the pillar of respect for people. The evidence that mutual respect and shared responsibility do enable higher levels of performance comes from every RIE, starting with the diversity of the teams, the fact that hierarchy vanishes in the RIE and that improvement occurs. Allowing and expecting anyone to stop a process to prevent a defect from moving forward is another great example of this concept.

5

Lean Tool Box

Any high-quality tool box has an array of tools that enables the completion of excellent, professionally done work in the face of differing tasks or changing situations. The Lean tool box is no exception to this concept, but it even goes above that high bar. Many components of the Lean tool box are delineated in Table 5.1.

The tools are simple to understand and easy to use, thus no worker is excluded from their use, reflecting Toyota's commitment to respect for people. There are tools that facilitate prioritization and alignment of your organizational activities, tools that let you see the waste, tools that help you eliminate the waste, tools for quality, tools for design, and tools that enable a structured disciplined approach to Lean implementation. Many of the tools are so versatile that they can be used at multiple organizational levels, from the 30,000-foot level to the front line. We do not discuss every Lean tool, but rather focus on those we have found most helpful in our Lean journey. The reader who wishes to go deeper into the tools can find a larger array of Lean tools in the other references (Koenigsaecker, 2013).

TOOLS TO CREATE PRIORITIZATION AND ALIGNMENT

The concept of True North and the transformation plan of care (TPOC; Simpler Business System®) approach are used together to create organizational prioritization and alignment.

True North

Any successful journey requires knowledge not only of where you are headed, but also clarity regarding how to confirm where you are at any

TABLE 5.1

Lean Tool Box

Tools for Prioritization and Alignment	Tools for Quality
True North	Standard work
Transformation Plan of Care	Poka yoke
Value Streams	Andon
	Visual management
Tools for Seeing Waste	Quality checks
5 Whys	
Waste walk	**Tools for Structure**
Spaghetti diagram	Rapid improvement events
Communication circle	A3
Takt time and cycle time	
First pass yield	**Tools for Design**
Process mapping	3P
Seven tools of quality	2P
	Vertical value stream
Tools for Eliminating Waste	
5S	
Standard work	
Poka yoke (mistake proofing)	
Jidoka	
Andon (signal)	
One piece flow	
Kanban	
Quick changeover	
Level loading	
Flow cell	
Visual management	

given time and when you have arrived at your goal. As Yogi Berra said, "You've got to be very careful. If you don't know where you are going, you might not get there" (Berra, 2001). An organization's ultimate destination has been dubbed True North in Lean parlance. It reflects your mission, overarching goals, and institutional imperatives. In a real sense, it is the organization's heart and soul. For this reason, it is important that every leader's personal True North aligns with the organization's True North. If this alignment does not exist, a leader will struggle to achieve a deep commitment to the organization and there will be less joy in the work.

The path to True North should be laid out in the organization's strategic plan. The strategic plan is then woven into the framework of Lean activities using this array of tools.

EXERCISE

If your organization doesn't have a True North statement, begin to develop one. If you think you have one, go out into several work areas and ask 15–25 random employees with different roles, "What is our organization's True North (ultimate goal)?" If the answers are not what you think is the organization's True North, you should rethink either the True North statement or how it has been disseminated.

Write out your personal True North statement. See if it aligns with the organization's True North.

Transformation Plan of Care (Simpler Business System®)

Caring for a complex healthcare system that needs "treatment" is the same as caring for a complex patient who needs treatment. Ideally, you would not start by randomly ordering tests, performing procedures, and beginning therapies for the patient. You would obtain the details of the patient's history, develop a problem list, and create a differential diagnosis and a robust plan of care. Similarly, a plan of care should be part of the Lean approach to treating your health system's woes. Therefore, it is no surprise that in Lean implementation, a TPOC concept exists (Simpler Business System).

However, just as interns may not think through the plan of care in the structured way that a seasoned clinician would, those beginning the Lean journey may jump into using the tools without an overarching plan to use them effectively. In fact, during Denver Health's initial two years of its Lean journey, the TPOC was somewhat unstructured. Our learning suggests it would be best to have a seasoned Lean sensei (master teacher) help you develop a robust TPOC at the beginning of the organization's Lean journey. The TPOC, like a patient care plan, needs to be assessed at regular intervals to determine if the plan is being implemented, is achieving intended goals, or needs to be redone as conditions change.

This process of establishing your True North, developing the strategic plan, and creating a process by which Lean can facilitate implementing the strategy for reaching True North can be part of a Lean process called Hoshin Kanri, Hoshin planning, or policy or strategy deployment (Koenigsaecker, 2013; Marchwinski, Shook, and Schroeder, 2008). Hoshin planning also involves the cascading of the plan down into the organization and receiving feedback back up the information chain (Jackson, 2006).

The TPOC process at Denver Health developed into a yearly event that preceded the board and leadership retreats, which in turn preceded budget development. The event was one-day long and involved the executive team and was facilitated by a seasoned sensei. The process began with a review of the mission and the overarching institutional goals. Then, one or two system level measures for the central Lean outcome domains of quality, cost/productivity, human development, service/access, and growth that would confirm achievement of those goals were selected by the group. These were placed on the vertical axis of the TPOC matrix (Figure 5.1). These measures could change from year to year. These were prioritized by the executive staff who assigned a numerical weight of 1–5 to each system measure category (5 having the greatest weight). The organizational components such as the OR, the Emergency Department, Community Health, and Pharmacy were placed on the horizontal axis. The Executive Staff assigned a rank order (1–5, 5 being highest) to each component based on its impact on the system level measures. For example, the potential for the OR to have an impact on nosocomial infections likely would be given a 5. The weight was multiplied by the ranking. The values in each Rank × Weight (R × W) column were added ("Total" line in Figure 5.1). The areas with the highest totals were potential value streams for the next 12 months.

EXERCISE

Ask your executive team to write a paragraph on the process by which your organization selects (and deselects) areas for focused effort in the upcoming year. Have they all described the same process? Is your process driven by achieving financial, quality, and human development metrics that lead to True North?

Value Streams

The areas of focus identified in the TPOC become the organization's value streams (VSs). These areas reflect the organization's core business but they are narrow enough to provide focus. The identification of VSs involves both selection and deselection: only some processes will get intense focus. Both words in "value stream" are important. The customer defines the value and the providers/organization produce the value (Joint Commission Resources, 2006). The stream is the sequence of all steps in the process that creates the final product or deliverable. The steps should flow like a lovely uninterrupted stream being pulled to the ocean: no boulders, no rapids,

Core Components of the Enterprise

Outcome	Measure	Weight	Rank	R × W	Rank	R × W	Rank	R × W	Rank	R × W	Rank	R × W	Rank	R × W	Rank	R × W
Quality	Hypertension															
Quality	Nosocomial Infection															
Cost/ Productivity	Cost/Adjusted Discharge															
Human Development	Voluntary Turnover															
Service/Access	Divert															
Service/Access	Total Users															
Growth	Cash/Unduplicated User															
Growth	Net Income															
	Total	■		■		■		■		■		■		■		
	Rank											■		■		

FIGURE 5.1

Transformation plan of care (TPOC) for ranking components of the organization for value stream identification.

no required portages. In reality, every VS has boulders, rapids, and portages (barriers and workarounds). There are value-added and non-value-added steps in every VS. An important aspect of the work of Lean is to minimize or eliminate the non-value-added steps.

The VSs in manufacturing appear more obvious than in healthcare. At the highest level, from our patients' perspective, the two prime values we should deliver are maintaining or restoring health. Herein lies a dilemma in healthcare: "What are the VSs in a healthcare organization at an operational level?" The VSs should represent the critical components. These should be neither too big nor too small, which is much easier to say than do. One of Denver Health's first VSs was hospital flow, which was similar to striving to achieve world peace. We learned more focus was needed in establishing the breadth of a VS. Because picking VSs is hard, we have seen organizations avoiding this component and diving into random processes or tool usage. This approach may yield some process improvement and lure the leadership into continuing this random approach. We, as well as other Lean leaders, believe this is a mistake, limiting the power of Lean to create flow in key processes.

The number of VSs chosen from the TPOC exercise for the year depends on the organization's capacity, people resources, and desired pace. The areas that we finally established at the TPOC were dictated in part by the readiness and the leadership of a given area. Denver Health began with five VSs and within a year increased to 14 VSs. The VSs for 2012 are listed in Table 5.2.

TABLE 5.2

Denver Health 2012 Value Streams

Community Health Services (2)
Managed Care
Behavioral Health Services
Rocky Mountain Poison and Drug Center (2)
Obstetrics and Gynecology Service
Emergency Department and Adult Urgent Care
Clinical Care Process
Human Resources
Perioperative Services
Pharmacy
Specialty Clinics
Nursing
Supply Chain (Seasoned VS functioning without facilitator)
Paramedics (Seasoned VS functioning without facilitator)
HIT (converted to project status)

At the beginning of our journey, occasionally a leader in an area asked, "Why are we being picked as a VS? Do you think something is wrong with our area?" However, very soon we faced the opposite question with leaders asking, "Why aren't we a VS?"

As you would expect, some VSs remained year after year (revenue cycle, for example). However, some were "retired" as formal VSs such as supply chain, paramedics, and health information technology (HIT). The first two were mature, narrow enough in focus, and had Denver Health (DH) Black Belts in leadership roles. As such, they could continue to function as a VS with targets and reporting. However, they didn't require an assigned facilitator, who was the individual from the Lean systems improvement department whose primary role was to support VSs and rapid improvement events (RIEs). HIT was entering a major install that had more of a project dimension. For the size and complexity of our integrated system, it seemed that between 15 and 20 VSs would have been the ideal number in order to maximize the benefit of Lean. Our main limitation in achieving the higher number was the number of the executive staff members and our commitment to have an executive staff sponsor for each VS. We learned that two was the maximum number of VSs that any executive staff member could manage and that one was ideal. We also learned that a VS could not be assigned randomly to any executive staff member; the VS needed to be in their span of control.

Not every healthcare organization has the same structure, issues, resources, or leadership, therefore not all organizations will have the same VSs. However, similarities do exist in comparable healthcare organizations. Therefore, it is likely that similar types of organizations will have some VSs in common. For example, healthcare delivery systems should consider revenue cycle, supply chain, and perioperative services as VSs as they are likely related to the core business, and yield early high return on investment.

EXERCISE

What do you think would be likely candidates for your first VSs? Why have you chosen those? Do they link strategically to your system metrics and your True North?

Once you have established the VSs with your TPOC, you will need to establish executive sponsors, VS steering committees, define the metrics/deliverables for the VSs, and perform VS mapping. The VS map is a picture of all the steps in the process from the first to the last step in the VS.

These steps are discussed in detail in the "Tools for Structure" section of this chapter. The metrics for the individual VSs should drive to the system metrics and cascade to the RIEs and the results of these events will provide insights back to senior management.

TOOLS TO SEE WASTE

We are surrounded by waste, but we get so used to seeing the same things every day that we miss the waste that is around us. Many of you have probably seen the YouTube® video in which you were asked to count the ball passes among the team members wearing white. During the game a gorilla walks across the screen among the team members. Often the first time people see the video, they miss the gorilla because their focus was on counting the passes; we see what we focus on. Some people will insist that the gorilla wasn't there (they must have switched videos, as they would never miss something like that). Similarly, some people will insist that their processes have no waste because it is not the focus of their attention.

We need to change our glasses, get new lenses to see the waste and focus on seeing it. If you are a clinician, you probably can remember the first couple of times you saw a chest x-ray and then read the report and wondered, "How did the radiologist see that?" You then trained your eye and could see what was described (or at least some of it).

Lean has tools that enable us to see waste; these are listed in Table 5.1. Without everyone, especially the leadership, learning to see waste there can be no Lean journey. Some of the tools are specific to Lean such as the 5 whys and the waste walk. Other tools are used in other improvement methods such as the Pareto analysis or fishbone diagram. In regard to the latter point, as more sophisticated tools are developed for complex processes, there is no reason that they cannot be employed in the Lean framework.

5 Whys

Some readers may be familiar with the book, *All I Really Need to Know I Learned in Kindergarten* (Fulghum, 2003). The 5 whys get back that questioning mind that we had as children. A Toyota vice president was once asked about the secret of Toyota's success and his surprising answer was, "It is called five-why. We ask why five times" (Liker, 2004). An experienced

Lean sensei has said that "90 percent of all quality problems can be solved just by … asking why five times" (Koenigsaecker, 2013). Pretty impressive for something so simple. The 5 whys can be used in a variety of ways and on several levels. The 5 whys "peel the onion" on a process or a problem.

The 5 whys are asking us not to accept the frequent responses to the question, "Why are you doing it that way?" with "Because that is the way we always have done it," or "Because that is the rule," or "Because my resident told me that is how to do it," and even the trusted academic response, "Because the literature says so." Each of these deserves not just the first "why," but four more in order to reach the core reason for the approach. Often, it becomes clear that there is no good reason it is done that way. This is when improving the process can begin. This is very much like the process clinicians use to get to the root cause of a patient's chief complaint. When a patient comes to a provider and says her head hurts, the provider asks, "Why do you think your head hurts?" When the patient said she fell, the provider asks, "Why did you fall?" We follow the trail to the diagnosis.

The 5 whys can be used for high-level issues such as building a new wing of a hospital or becoming an accountable care organization (ACO) or a frontline issue such as the registration process.

EXERCISE

Think back over the last week. Was there some process that either didn't make sense or seemed to be a problem? What do you think the answers would have been if you asked "the 5 whys"?

Given that many hospitals have intermittent issues with divert, this is a great place to try out the 5 whys. Often an exchange can go like this: "We just went on divert."

First why: Why did we go on divert?
First answer: We had no beds.

Second why: Why did we have no beds?
Second answer: There have been no discharges yet today.

Third why: Why have there been no discharges yet today?
Third answer: The residents haven't written the discharge orders yet.

Fourth why: Why haven't the residents written the discharges yet?
Fourth answer: They are still on attending rounds.

Fifth why: Why didn't they write the orders before attending rounds?
Fifth answer: No one has told them to do that.

Now you can begin to explore a solution to that problem.

Occasionally you might need a few more "whys" to get to the real diagnosis. Some sensei suggest that the 5 whys be followed by 5 hows in order to suggest possible ways to fix the root cause (Cooper, 2011). The 5 whys and the 5 hows help us avoid jumping to fixes without utilizing the other Lean tools that help us address the root causes of problems.

Waste Walk

The waste walk is an integral part of the Lean concept of going to where the work is done (going to the *gemba*), or as we say, to the place where the truth is found. A waste walk, like many of the Lean tools, is quite simple; have a group of individuals, usually those not involved in the process, watch a process with "new eyes" through a Lean lens. This brings to mind another profound Yogi Berra observation, "You can observe a lot by just watching" (Berra, 2001). As with many of Yogi Berra's quips, this makes a lot of sense, but like so many things in life that are common sense, this careful observing is not so common. The power of patiently and carefully observing was so important to Toyota that new hires on their first day of work were asked to spend the day inside a small chalk circle (called the *Ohno* circle after the Toyota leader who established it) observing the work (Liker, 2004). Would it not be a great idea for every new employee in healthcare to stand and watch the work that she was going to be doing? If her supervisor watched with her, think of what we could all learn.

When you conduct a waste walk, it is respectful to the employees in the area to be informed that the waste walk team is coming. As you do waste walks regularly, everyone gets used to this, but in the beginning it can be intimidating, especially when you are the CEO on a team doing a waste walk!

In a waste walk every observer gets a list of the eight wastes. Then the team sets off to the site of the process and just watches for about an hour, filling in the list with details of the observed wastes. While on the walk, the team should get input from the employees in the area and from customers. For example, if you are watching a clinic process, talking to the patients in the waiting room lets you get their perspective on the process. However, the observers should not alter the workflow. At the end of the walk, all the observers should thank the employees and the team should compare notes. This provides information on which wastes need to be targeted in order to develop a new and better process. The waste walk can occur any time, but we always used it as one of the first activities of an RIE. When it is done as part of an RIE, the observed wastes inform the current state process map. Table 5.3 illustrates the many

TABLE 5.3

Wastes Found in Waste Walk in Community Health Asthma Care RIE

Underutilized Human Talent

Not using spirometry to fullest capacity
PCPs not permitted to interpret spirometry; delayed care

Waiting

Calibration takes time
Waiting for spirometer to turn on
Have to calibrate machine with first use every day
Wait time for room with machine if occupied
Waiting for printout

Inventory

Cost of disposables in inventory

Transportation

Spirometry not centrally located
Need to go to multiple rooms; may need to wait for room or spirometer
Taking patient to another room for vital signs before taking patient to do pulmonary
  function test (PFT)

Defects

No log book to record last spirometer calibration
Temperature must be input; may not be readily available
Don't have medication needed on hand; using another medication that takes longer
Need thermometer in room to enter temperature into machine
Spirometer does not interface with electronic record
Lack of interface with electronic health record
"Manually" cleaning up spirometry data
Machine has more capability than we use (but could use)
Calibration has to be done several times

Motion

Patient moves a couple of times (vital signs, spirometry, exam room)
Patient needs to go to machine versus machine going to the patient

Overproduction

More printout than what you need
More information on PFT report than we need

Overprocessing

Having to manually delete patient from list
Paper for machine and mouth pieces
Manual input of patient demographics/info
Redundancy: have to enter information in several places

wastes that a team found in a process during a waste walk. We have maintained the categories of waste that the team used. However, as we indicated earlier, the categories are not as critical as is the identification of the wastes.

EXERCISE

Ask the next nurse manager or surgeon or anesthesiologist you hire to stand in the middle of a hospital floor or operating room board, respectively, and observe the process for an hour (we won't go as far as Toyota and ask for a whole day). Using a list of the eight wastes, have the person list the wastes he sees. Have him share this list with his work team.

Spaghetti Diagram

A spaghetti diagram is one of those tools that make you love Lean. It is so simple to do and it communicates the problems of wasted motion or transportation dramatically. Everyone gets it immediately (it may be helpful to be Italian or to be an Italian food lover)! A spaghetti diagram is a picture of the physical path that a worker, patient, or equipment/device follows to get the job done. In its simplest form, it shows movement; it can be refined to document steps or distances.

To do the mapping, start by going to the area where the process is occurring and draw a picture of the area. This can be a rough hand-drawn picture and does not need to be drawn to scale. Each observer should be assigned to watch a different person in the process and each observer is given a different colored pen to distinguish the movements of the person she is watching from the movement of the others. For example, if you are mapping a process in a clinic, someone should be drawing the movements of the clerk, someone else the nurse, someone else the healthcare partner, and so on. Each person's movement is drawn in a different color. The initial spaghetti diagram becomes the foundation for the next step, which is to begin to eliminate wasted movement, getting rid of most of the spaghetti. Figure 5.2 is a spaghetti diagram from a clinic RIE. The RIE team reduced the wasteful movement by 5S'ing the rooms, standardizing room supplies, and creating parallel work rather than sequential work of the team. As illustrated in Figure 5.2, putting the before and after pictures side by side is a powerful reinforcement for the power of Lean to remove waste.

In general, we have thought so little about the workflow design in healthcare, that when you map almost any process, it looks like a big plate

Before   After

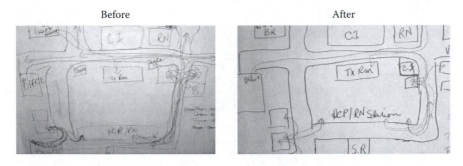

FIGURE 5.2
Spaghetti diagrams before and after removing wasteful movement.

of spaghetti. Although a plate of spaghetti might make your mouth water, seeing a process mapped as a spaghetti diagram might make you cry.

EXERCISE

Have someone from your quality department or mid-manager group do a spaghetti diagram by following the clerk's, the floor nurse's, and intern's steps in getting a patient ready for discharge from the time it is decided until the patient leaves the hospital unit. It might be a fun twist to give them pedometers and have them guess in advance the number of steps it will take to accomplish this.

Communication Circle

Many errors that affect patient safety and quality are the result of inadequate communication. We know that many of the barriers to smooth efficient flow are issues with communication. Two common examples of this are:

Delay in getting a patient from the emergency department to an inpatient bed often occurs because providers are waiting for communication about bed availability, nursing report, or physician orders.
Failure to rescue a deteriorating patient can occur because of convoluted and nonstandardized processes for nurses' and physicians' communication.

The communication circle brings the complexity of the communication into the light of day. A communication circle is basically a spaghetti diagram of the movement of information and is always just as messy as the movement of people. The communication circle lets you see quickly how inefficient the flow of information is. Figure 5.3 is a before and after picture of the communication circles generated by an RIE team that was addressing

Before   After

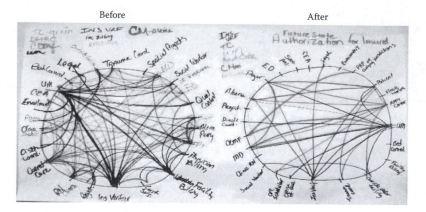

FIGURE 5.3

Inpatient to outpatient services referral communication circles before and after removing wasteful communication.

the patient authorization process for posthospital discharge specialist referral. The "before" communication circle revealed the possibility of 81 information handoffs in the authorization process, depending on third-party payer requirements. The team developed standard work for utilization managers, specialty clinic staff, and appointment center coordinators, and submitted six IT enhancements, reducing the number of potential handoffs to 29. Putting the "after" communication circle from the new process next to the previous communication circle lets you see the improvement.

Exercise

Repeat the above spaghetti diagram of the discharge of a patient now with lines of communication to create a communication circle.

Takt Time and Cycle Time

Time may be our least renewable resource. Therefore, when we think of waste, wasting time has to be an important focus of Lean. Takt time and cycle time, not surprisingly given the names, are time measurements.

Takt Time

Takt time interestingly is a German word (not Japanese) that crept into the Lean vocabulary and means a precise time interval such as a musical meter (Marchwinski et al., 2008). The Germans first used the concept as a management tool in their aircraft industry (Marchwinski et al.,

2008). This suggests that work, like music, has a required rhythm. Takt time is calculated by dividing the available time by the demand, such as the number of times a service is performed per day (Marchwinski et al., 2008). For example, if the pharmacy operates 600 minutes per day filling prescriptions, and the pharmacy needs to fill 300 prescriptions a day (the demand), the takt time is two minutes per prescription (Joint Commission Resources, 2008). This calculation does not tell you if the actual process of filling the prescription takes one, two, or five minutes, but it does begin to provide insight into whether the pharmacy can accomplish the work required using the current process to meet the patient care demand.

This seems very simple, but it can be tricky. For example, let's think about the operating room. You could calculate your takt time by year, by month or by week, but these calculations may not be sufficiently granular to help you understand the flow. The shorter the period of time you use, the more helpful the measurement. In the operating room example, calculating takt time for periods of 7 a.m. to 3 p.m., 3 p.m. to 11 p.m., and 11 p.m. to 7 a.m. would likely be more helpful because this more accurately reflects the flow of patients. Similarly, calculating the takt time for the case type (ophthalmology, orthopedics, neurosurgery, etc.) would also provide more useful data as these cases clearly require differing amounts of time due to their varying complexity. Takt time is an important starting place for understanding patient demand, the process flow, and staffing needs but it is an underused (or never used) concept in healthcare. Calculation of takt time leads you to the next step, which is to determine how long the process is actually taking, which is the cycle time.

Cycle Time

Cycle time is the observation of the actual time it takes to complete a specific process (Marchwinski et al., 2008). In the pharmacy example, it would be how long it takes the pharmacist to fill a prescription. In our pharmacy example, if the takt time is two minutes and the cycle time is four minutes then you have an intrinsic process problem that will prevent your meeting patient demand. Thus, these measurements focus your first effort on getting your cycle time to equal your takt time for the particular patient flow. One step in achieving this is to use these measurements to inform staffing needs. When cycle time is divided by takt time, you can determine the number of people who are needed for the task. The pharmacy would need two pharmacists to meet the demand (four divided by two).

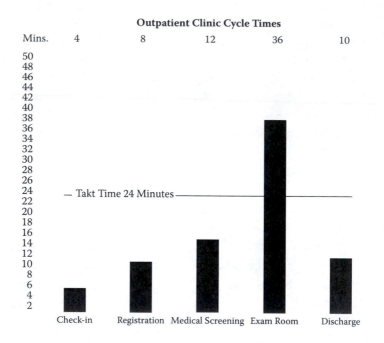

FIGURE 5.4

Cycle time bar chart.

Figures 5.4 and 5.5 are taken from an outpatient clinic RIE. The cycle time bar chart shown in Figure 5.4 depicts patient flow in the clinic. The vertical bars represent the cycle times for the main processes in a visit. The horizontal line represents the takt time, which was calculated by dividing the available time in one provider session (4 hours, or 240 minutes by the 10 scheduled visits/session (patient demand)(240 minutes/10 Patients = Takt time of 24 minutes).

In an ideal manufacturing setting, operating at this takt time, a completed car would come off the assembly line every 24 minutes and a new car would enter. In the ideal clinic, a "completed patient" should exit the clinic every 24 minutes and a new patient begin a visit. In order for this smooth flow to occur, no step in the process can exceed the takt time. If that happens, patients would back up behind that step. The cycle time bar chart in Figure 5.4 depicts just that situation. Moreover, it is important to note that while the steady state flow has patients entering and exiting every 24 minutes, an individual patient visit time is longer than the takt time, reflecting the total time of all the steps. All steps must have the waste removed to reduce the patient visit time.

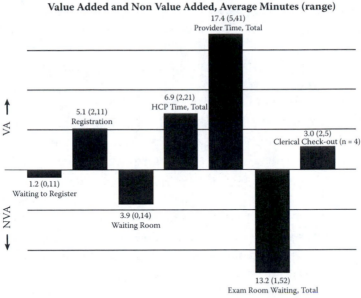

FIGURE 5.5
Cycle time bar chart for value-added (VA) and non-value-added (NVA) time.

Figure 5.5 displays the times for each step as the total value-added (VA) and non-value-added (NVA) time. This allows the team to see where the NVA time occurred during the visit. Surprisingly, the greatest amount of NVA time occurred in the exam room: it was being used as an extension of the waiting room. The goal of this RIE was to eliminate NVA steps and to have all VA steps operating at or slightly below takt time. Because the time the patient spent in the exam room was above takt time, the team focused there. Three clear problems were observed: the provider entered and exited the exam room up to four times; there was overreliance on face-to-face communication among staff, creating delays; and the staff was not prepared for varying patient complexity. To address these issues, the team implemented care team huddles prior to clinic sessions to "scrub" upcoming schedules and prepare for patients with the greatest number of needs; designed and implemented a flow management board providing a visual queue for communicating to patients estimated wait time, and allowing staff to flex to assist when needed; improved the standard work associated with the use of exam room flags, and created standard work and care team communication boxes to facilitate the right person doing the right job and reduce the need for face-to-face communication.

The cycle time bar graph also shows that the check-in, registration, medical screening, and discharge processes were operating below takt time, indicating that the people performing these functions have unused time. The team identified tasks that could be reassigned to these steps to distribute needed work more evenly.

Therefore, this type of visualization can help in redesigning a process. One caution in the use of takt time and cycle time is that if the patient flow is not smooth (which it is usually not) throughout the period of any process involving patients, patient waiting will occur even if overall average takt time and average cycle time are equal. In our pharmacy example, if most patients arrived at nine in the morning, demand would exceed capacity at that point in time and patient waits would occur. There are several standard approaches to address this issue. The first is to make the takt granular as in the operating room discussion. The second approach, used in manufacturing, is to aim for a cycle time that is slightly shorter than takt time to accommodate variation. The third approach is to smooth the flow. For example, in the operating room discussion, one approach to smoothing the flow is not to schedule elective surgeries preferentially on Monday, but to more evenly distribute the workload.

First Pass Yield

First pass yield is a quality measurement. It is a measure of how often the process occurs with no defects. In our pharmacy example of 300 prescriptions, if all of them were correct in all aspects, the first pass yield would be 100% which, of course, would be the ideal state. This would be something we would value in healthcare; certainly, the patients would. Yet, it is a measurement we rarely use and, probably, we rarely achieve 100% first pass yield. Focus on first pass yield clearly improves quality and can have a positive financial impact by reducing rework.

Example

The Rocky Mountain Poison and Drug Center conducted an RIE to evaluate the use of standard work to ensure an efficient quality process and decrease unnecessary corrections by applying the Lean concept of quality at the source. As a baseline they measured the first pass yield of one process and found it to be 54%. The event demonstrated that individual performance metrics were not communicated and that the quality check list was not being utilized (standard work was not being followed). Through a series of rapid experiments in the event week, they eliminated a number of non-value-added steps and implemented self-checks of quality, created level loading of work, as well as a number of other process changes. The results targeted a 90% first pass yield and eliminated the need for a new clerical position.

EXERCISE

Do you know the takt time, cycle time, and first pass yield of any of the core processes in your areas of responsibility?

PROCESS MAPPING

Process mapping is a tool that creates a visual representation of the key steps in a workflow. It is a critical tool in identifying waste. There is no substitute for using this tool. To be a meaningful process map, it must be based on direct observation, not on what people describe the process to be. These two descriptions rarely are the same. A complete process map includes the sequence of all work steps as well as the flow of information and supplies. Many methodologies exist for process mapping, but there are at least four important and somewhat unique aspects in Lean process mapping. The first is the identification of not only the workflow steps, but also the barriers to that flow. The second is that the flow is from the customer's perspective. The third is that in using processing mapping in Lean, not only is the current process mapped but also the target/future state is mapped. Finally, the ideal state is mapped to provide an ultimate, far-reaching goal. The use of an ideal state map in Lean underscores that the new future state is not about minor corrections in what you are doing now but is about creating process breakthroughs that yield substantial improvements.

Lean process mapping may be used at various levels of granularity: a 10,000-ft level view that would be the VS map or a frontline process which would be used in an RIE. There are a few differences in the actual map and the specific use of the map between a VS and an RIE process map. A key outcome of a VS map is to identify the major barriers to flow that can become the focus of individual RIEs. A key outcome of an RIE process map is to identify NVA steps to eliminate.

A process map of patient flow for scheduled (nonemergency) orthopedic surgery could be the high-level map for the orthopedic service line.

This level map could equate to a VS map. The team would capture all of the steps from the time the physician in the orthopedic clinic requests scheduling surgery through the time the patient is discharged from the postoperative unit. Mapping would likely also be done for the component processes within the VS such as the actual steps for scheduling the elective surgical procedure. This would be the scope for an RIE. In either case, the primary objective is to identify the wastes within the process being mapped that prevent flow from occurring on demand without waste.

There is a variety of tools, icons, and symbols used by process mapping engineers. We found that the simplest tools and approaches have advantages. We used multiple colored sticky notes and markers to denote the steps in the process and placed the sticky notes on a large piece of butcher-block paper (30 in. top to bottom) to create a picture/map of the process. You may be asking "Isn't there an 'app' for that?" The answer is, of course, "Yes." There are electronic mapping software options but for the money (no wasteful spending), sticky notes are a great choice. Teams are amazed with the output and understanding they can generate using nothing but sticky notes and markers. In contrast, we found teams utilizing electronic formatting spent more time on formatting than they did identifying the wastes and it tends to exclude the less technically savvy people (a conflict with respect for people).

A full description of the various icons and symbols that can be used in process mapping can be found in a number of references (Marchwinski et al., 2008; Rother and Shook, 2003). In our simplistic "sticky note" approach, a yellow sticky is a process step; a blue sticky is for trigger and for done; a pink sticky is used to mark points in the process for meaningful incremental improvement or potential RIEs; a sticky on its side, a diamond, is a decision point. The primary objective is to have a legend that everyone understands.

Mapping healthcare processes takes time. A complete VS mapping including identification of the components that will be the eight to ten RIEs in the next year takes three to four days. The process for the scope of an RIE takes about a day. The use of this tool should follow the steps outlined next and not be rushed.

Step 1: The first job of the team is identifying the primary customer inasmuch as the customer defines the value-added components. This should be the patient. As discussed above, the processes also have other internal and external customers, but they should not be defining value-added and non-value-added components of the process.

Step 2: The next step in mapping is deciding what process you are actually mapping. You will need to identify your starting (called the trigger) and end points (surprisingly dubbed, done); sounds obvious and easy. But, it is not as easy as it might appear. For example, when does registration begin: when the patient arrives at the clinic or when the registration clerk enters the first keystroke? When is it done: when the final keystroke is entered, when an armband is placed on the patient, or when the copayment is collected? A team member's job and her perspective can influence these decisions. You will not be able to measure accurate time observations of the process until your team reaches decisions on these simple, but deceivably difficult to define, timestamps.

Step 3: The next step is to identify all the steps in the process between trigger and done. Each step should include a noun and a verb. For example, rather than identifying a step as "Scheduling" the activity should be identified as "patient calls for appointment." This description of the process step starts to open the "process black box." Then, seeing the steps through the patient's eyes, red dots are placed on the yellow sticky notes that represent non-value-added steps (waste) and a green dot is placed on sticky notes that are value-added steps, something for which the patient would be willing to pay. Clearly, seeing the provider gets a green dot and sitting in the waiting room gets a red dot. Opportunities for improvement become readily apparent. Get rid of those red dots!

The best mapping process uses data blocks under each process step to delineate key attributes of the step using data from the application of Lean tools. For example, the data block in an RIE map could include cycle time, first pass yield, and the top three defects that mark that step.

Step 4: This step uses the information gleaned in Step 3 to create the target or future state map that eliminates those red dots through creation of improved process flow.

There are a number of operational Lean approaches to eliminate the red dots: Just Do Its, RIEs, and projects. The "Just Do Its" are precisely that: go fix it now. They are tasks that can be done by one person in a day. In our method for VS mapping the pink stickies mark a point where an RIE could be used to remove those red dots. For an ideal transformational pace, there should be eight to ten RIEs identified in each VS to be

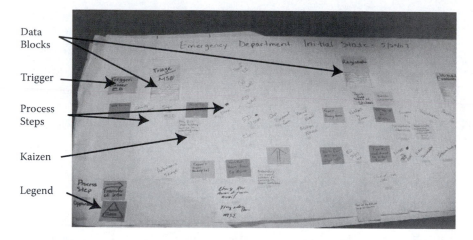

Data Blocks

Trigger

Process Steps

Kaizen

Legend

FIGURE 5.6
Part of a value stream map for emergency department.

performed over 12 months. If mapping a VS, there should be identification of the metrics, roles, and responsibilities and schedule of the Lean activities. Although projects can emerge from VS mapping, we tried to avoid the project mode except for obviously complex, large initiatives such as health information technology (HIT) installments or constructing a new facility.

Remember that a process map is a time-limited document. Removing waste changes the map. Given the pace of eight to ten RIEs per year, we found that VSs needed to be remapped yearly. Also, it is important to realize it takes four to five passes at a specific VS to remove a majority of the non-value-added steps (Koenigsaecker, 2013).

Figure 5.6 is one section of the current-state VS map for the emergency department VS. This portion of the map details the front-end process, for both ambulatory patients and for patients arriving by ambulance. The key for the icons is in the lower left-hand corner. Two RIEs (out of a total of eight RIEs identified for this VS for the year) were identified from this VS map focusing on the ED registration process and the medical screening process.

Process maps for some RIEs are shown in Figures 5.7 through 5.9. Figure 5.7 is the current state map for patient bed assignment (bed pull) to the adult inpatient behavioral health unit. Using the waste walk the team identified many of the eight wastes including:

Wait time after accepting patient >30 minutes
Waiting for security

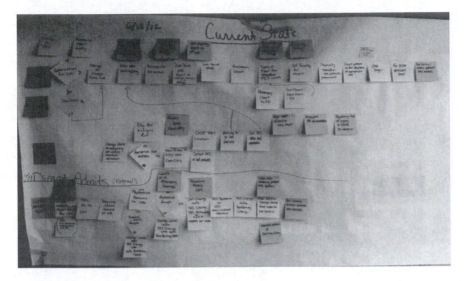

FIGURE 5.7
Bed pull processing map for behavioral health services.

Delays in entering patient into information system
Physically having to transfer admit order to bed control off hours
Documentation for valuables not complete when transferring
Unproductive back and forth phone calling
Duplication of RN work when admitting during change of shift
Not accepting report on first call/not carrying mobile phone

The process map that emerged identified several major barriers to flow marked with pink stickies (the darker stickies in the picture). These barriers included:

Direct admits were always not prioritized when the psychiatric ED became overloaded.
There was inconsistent use of standard work for inpatient bed pull.
The use of our computerized bed tracking system was inconsistent and suboptimal in the psychiatric units.

Addressing these became a central focus of the RIE.

Figure 5.8 was the current state map for the process for depositing the cash generated from the clinics from the previous day. The team mapped the process as two major flows: the physical handling of the cash and the process of data entry and accounting. One might consider cash handling

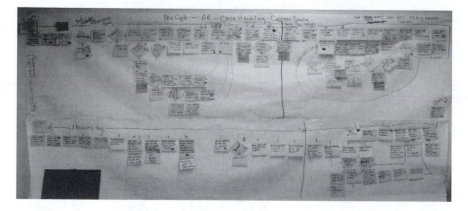

FIGURE 5.8
Revenue cycle cash handling process map.

a simple process: you take in cash and deposit it in the bank. However, as is frequently the case, the waste walk and the mapping revealed a complex process vividly portrayed by all the stickies on this map. Some of the wastes included:

An average of five clinic deposits a day are submitted to cash handling with errors.
Significant amounts of time (from 1 hour up to several days) is spent fixing these errors.
The same error was being worked by multiple staff.
Multiple verification steps add little value.
Lack of standard work between cash handling and cash applications.
Existing policy for cash collection sites is not uniformly followed.
Silos of process knowledge.

In addition, barriers to smooth flow included numerous collection, deposits, and data entry sites. These wastes and the barriers to flow became the focus of the team's work.

Figure 5.9 displays the current state map from an RIE in the human resource VS for the employee corrective action process. This map illustrated delays and even "retrograde process flow" depicted by the large black arrows. The data collected for this event showed that lead times for simple verbal and written reprimands were 36 and 50 days. The RIE process allowed the team to shorten and improve the process significantly.

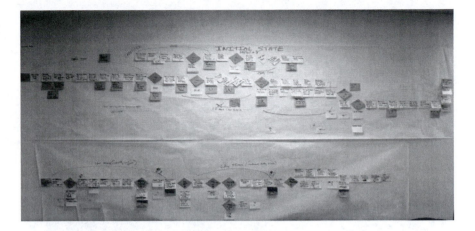

FIGURE 5.9
Human resource corrective actions process map.

SEVEN TOOLS OF QUALITY

Although Lean has some unique tools, Lean also uses other tried and true tools to help see waste. These other commonly used tools have been dubbed the "Seven Tools of Quality" or the "Seven Basic Tools" and are listed in Table 5.4 (Koenigsaecker, 2013). These tools fit well with Lean as they are visual representations of information and are generally easy to understand. We do not describe all of these in detail, but rather focus on those we found most helpful.

Fishbone

The fishbone diagram, also known as a cause and effect diagram and as the Ishikawa diagram for its original designer, received its name because it looks like the skeleton of a fish, but there is nothing fishy about its worth (Arthur, 2011).

TABLE 5.4

Seven Tools of Quality

Fishbone Diagram	Control Chart
Pareto Chart	Scatter Gram
Histogram	Check Sheet
Run Chart	

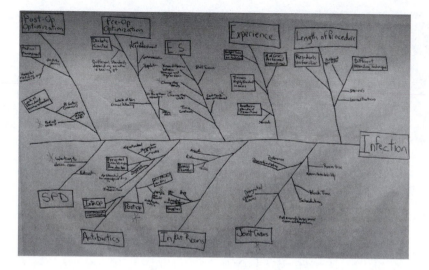

FIGURE 5.10
Fishbone diagram of perioperative infection control.

It is used to identify and sort causes that together produce an outcome. The "ribs" of the skeleton can be used to group specific issues into categories. In healthcare, some of the categories could be "orders, using supplies and medications, using equipment, using standard procedures, and environment" (Joint Commission Resources, 2008). In an RIE, the fishbone can be used in the early brainstorming phase and in the gap analysis. The beauty of the fishbone is that you see at a glance all the components that contribute to a specific outcome (in this case perioperative infection) and in what areas these components cluster. It doesn't tell you the relative frequency of each of these components. However, we have a tool for that, the Pareto chart.

The fishbone diagram shown in Figure 5.10 was adapted from the brainstorming in an RIE in the perioperative VS. As you can see, this is a "busy" fishbone. You will frequently see this, reflecting how dysfunctional many of our processes are. All of these issues could not be addressed in a weeklong RIE. Therefore, the team focused on those items they thought they could successfully address during that week (noted by the asterisk on the fishbone). In this way the tool can also be utilized for prioritization.

Pareto Chart

A Pareto chart is a simple bar graph of a size or frequency distribution of what you are observing. The vertical axis is frequency and the horizontal axis is the specific activity. The length of time over which the frequency is measured can vary depending on what you are observing. The bars go from the largest on the left to the smallest on the right so you can see the most common events easily. A line can be added on the chart that is the cumulative number moving from left to right, achieving 100% at the end. Joseph Juran named this graph after the Italian, Vilfredo Pareto, who observed in 1906 that 80% of the land in Italy was owned by 20% of the population (Juran, 1975). This observation has given rise to the other name for the graph, the 80–20 rule, reflecting that in many circumstances 80% of the variation comes from 20% of the causes or what Juran termed the "vital few and the trivial many" (Juran, 1975). An example of a Pareto chart, depicting the activities a nurse performs in a day, is shown in Figure 5.11. Although the largest amount of the nurses' time was spent in direct patient care, it was less than half of the total shift and the next largest amount of time was spent on charting. Of note, there appear to be many activities that would fall into one of the eight waste categories. The utility of the Pareto chart is it tells you at a glance where most of the

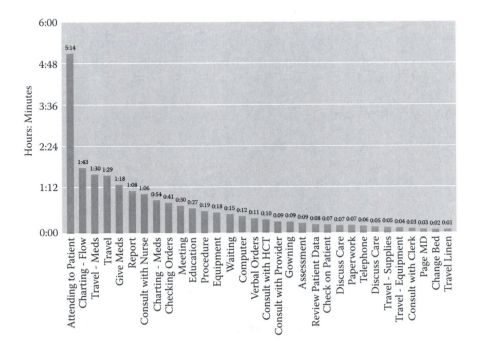

FIGURE 5.11
Pareto of trauma nurses' activities (24-hour observation).

activity is and can then direct your efforts to where you may "get the most bang for the buck."

Histograms, run charts, control charts, scatter grams, and check sheets are slightly more complex visual representations of certain aspects of processes that others have used as part of Lean (Koenigsaecker, 2013; Arthur, 2011).

TOOLS TO ELIMINATE WASTE

5S

The 5S is a foundational tool that reduces many of the eight wastes including waiting, transport, motion, inventory, and even defects through the disciplined creation of an organized visual workplace. The 5Ss refer to each component of the organizing sequence that begins with S in Japanese. As is shown in Figure 5.12, you can name them so that this is true in English as well. Different practitioners have translated the Japanese words slightly differently but they all begin with S. In recent years, some Lean experts have added a sixth S for safety (Koenigsaecker, 2013). Some have said there are really only 4Ss suggesting if you are doing it right, you can drop the last S for Sustain (Marchwinski et al., 2008).

The first S is Sort, which focuses on removing everything from the workplace that you do not use or need; that means everything. Even those items that are used infrequently should be placed away from the main workflow.

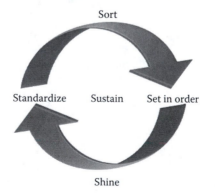

FIGURE 5.12
Components of 5S.

TABLE 5.5

Red Tag Information

Name of Item	Recommended Disposition
Inventory Control Number	Contact Person
Date Red-Tagged	Final Disposition by Date
Reason Tagged	

In our homes, most of us collect "stuff," thinking we may need it some time. My elderly mother saved every plastic bag! This tendency occurs at work as well. Because the healthcare workforce has a significant turnover, someone may have stashed forms, supplies, or equipment and then he or she left, but the stash remained. In many areas such as the operating rooms, the emergency department, an inpatient unit, or a clinic, individuals may be reluctant to get rid of an item they think someone else may need. 5S has an answer for this dilemma: red tags and Red Tag areas. As an area is being 5Sed such items can have a red tag, as shown in Table 5.5, with identifying information on it and the item placed in a designated Red Tag area. Some organizations include additional information on the red tag. Clearly, whatever the organization finds helpful can be added. The Red Tag area can be by floor, department, or for the entire organization. This Red Tag area can become the place for a type of organizational "garage sale." The items should be in a Red Tag area for a defined period of time and if no one provides a good reason for keeping an item by that time, it goes. Often these items can be donated to charitable organizations.

The second S is for Set in Order and is linked to the first S. Once the unneeded items have been discarded, the ones that are part of daily work need to be set in an order that facilitates their efficient use in the workflow. This step eliminates the waste of excess motion. A spaghetti diagram can help identify the least waste way for the space layout. It is often useful to mark with tape, paint, or another similar method exactly where a piece of equipment should go so that it doesn't "drift" into a place that makes its use inefficient.

Once unneeded supplies (either ones that aren't used or ones of which too many are onsite) have been removed, the remaining ones should be placed in bins or shelves that are clearly labeled. These are placed in an order so that the most used items are at eye level or in front. This will facilitate an inventory pull system described below. This is nicely illustrated in Figure 5.13. A clerk on one of the hospital floors put all the doctor's forms

FIGURE 5.13
Organization of doctors' forms as examples of 5S.

in specific spaces with labels preventing "hunting and gathering" time and creating an organized appearance.

The third S is for Shine and is also linked to the first two. Everything that remains and the space it is in should be sparkling clean. This facilitates employees seeing when something is abnormal (Cooper, 2011). From a patient and family perspective, all healthcare entities should embrace these first three Ss. It would not be reassuring for patients or their families to come into a room—whether it is an office, ED exam room, or an ICU—and see disorganization and dirt. Moreover, in a healthcare setting Shine should facilitate infection control by using the correct cleaning procedures for each piece of equipment and each area.

The fourth and fifth Ss are for Standardize and Sustain. They go together and oppose the underlying force of entropy: things move to chaos (a loose interpretation of this law of thermodynamics). We have all seen this in our garages; you clean it and six months later it is a mess again. Standardize and Sustain prevents this. In this context Standardize means "the method you use to maintain the first three 5S components (Productivity Press Development Team, 1996). A specific person, a time frequency, and a work process are assigned to keep the Sort, Set in Order, and Shine maintained. Just as checklists have become a tool in clinical medicine for standardizing, a 5S checklist can also be developed, used, and posted. A simple example of the utility of Standardize and Sustain occurred in the central store-room for the administrative suite at Denver Health. The area had been 5Sed many times but would always slide back toward disorganization: who knew how those old rolodexes kept coming back. Finally, the administrative assistants developed a checklist with one of them assigned each month to perform specific 5S components and then no slippage occurred. The laboratory department instituted a daily 5S at the beginning of the first shift (more on their effort in Chapter 7) and the department of medicine instituted a monthly 5S for administrative areas.

Sustain refers to "making a habit of maintaining the procedures" (Productivity Press Development Team, 1996). In some ways this melds with Standardize, but some experts would say that Standardize is process and Sustain is a personal and organizational commitment (Productivity Press Development Team, 1996).

5S'ing can be an individual or team sport: one person 5S'ing her office or an entire department 5S'ing their building. Although at first blush 5S may look like spring cleaning, a second look demonstrates that it is a disciplined and functional approach to organizing resources, space, and flow, and facilitates the implementation of standard work. 5S saves time, prevents errors, saves money, and respects workers by creating an environment that supports them. Its importance in creating a Lean enterprise is reflected in the fact that entire books have been written on just this simple tool (Productivity Press Development Team, 1996; Osada, 1991).

In manufacturing 5S has focused on physical space, but we had a broader view. We have considered not only macro but micro space and virtual space. We have focused on surgical procedure preference cards, 5S'ing what was on the operating room trays for individual procedures and at the same time standardizing them. We 5S'ed our computer storage and our procedures and practice policies (P&Ps). Clearly, when an organization does these areas, not all the Ss apply literally. However, one can certainly "scrub," if not shine what is in P&Ps and in computer files. Some seasoned Lean practitioners note a 15% increase in productivity in a manufacturing setting with this simple tool (Koenigsaecker, 2013). Denver Health realized significant financial benefits from 5S, which are detailed in Chapter 7.

Creating order in the workplace is so foundational to Lean that no organization that is serious about Lean should omit this process. The use of 5S as the beginning for Denver Health's Lean journey is detailed in Chapter 7.

EXERCISE

Go into your office. Take a look around. Are there any piles? Open up the cabinets and open up the drawers. Are there items you never use? Try 5S'ing. If you have an assistant, he can do his office at the same time: double your fun! If you want real fun, use a variant of 5S and organize your computer, starting with your e-mail!

Standard Work

The concept of standardizing to solve and improve (Simpler Business System®) that is discussed in Chapter 4 is built on the development of standard work. From the Toyota perspective standard work is a defined workflow that relies on observation and measurement of takt time, work sequence, individual work assignments, needed supplies, quality checks, and posting of the standard worksheet (Koenigsaecker, 2013; Joint Commission Resources, 2008).

The standard worksheet can serve at least three primary purposes: a detailed description of the work for the person doing it, documentation for a new employee to be used in training, and for visual management by supervisors who can observe if the standard work is actually being performed as expected.

Standard work is clearly lacking in most aspects of healthcare, but it is a foundational component of Lean. Even when standard work has been established, it is frequently not adhered to or even ignored. Again, think of your institution's compliance with hand hygiene, let alone the numerous protocols, algorithms, and clinical guidelines that exist but suffer from variable compliance. Although we did strive for establishing standard work in all the processes that we examined and improved, we did not include all the steps in the Toyota's posted standard work. We only described work sequences, individual work assignments, and needed supplies. We could have benefited from inclusion of all the information.

Poka Yoke, Jidoka, and Andon

These three tools represent a hierarchical and closely related sequence for preventing errors from occurring and having defects being sent on through a process. Because they are closely related it is not always clear in which bin a specific intervention lies. However, the key point is that one focus of Lean is to prevent errors from going through an entire process to the customer.

Poka Yoke

Poka yoke is a tool to prevent errors from ever happening and their consequent defects, thus, enabling quality at the source. Despite poka yoke having a catchy sound, it is truly deadly serious. Poka yoke, or mistake/error proofing, recognizes the fundamental reality of being human: even well-intentioned and well-trained people can and do make mistakes. The core construct of poka yoke is to have a method/device in place that ensures the proper conditions exist for the right outcome before executing the process. It allows everyone, even a novice, to work without making mistakes. Fortunately for us, many industries have embraced the concept. The next time you fill up your car with gas, in addition to being shocked by the price, notice the many poka yokes in this everyday process: the gas won't flow until you pay, the diesel nozzle won't fit into a car that uses unleaded gas, the gas stops flowing when the tank is 95% full, and gas stops flowing if the hose is ripped out of the pump (Koenigsaecker, 2013).

The fact that 100,000 people die per year from errors and many more are injured or experience near misses in American hospitals underscores the benefit that would accrue from mistake proofing (IOM, 1999). Fortunately, we do have examples where we have done mistake proofing:

A provider can't connect the oxygen flow meter to the room air wall outlet due to the design of the connections, as are shown in Figure 5.14, preventing a patient who needs oxygen from getting only room air through the tubing.

Similarly, a provider cannot connect the tubing that operates the sequential compression device that is used on patients' legs after surgery to the intravenous solution port.

A computerized order entry system can prevent the pharmacy providing the wrong dose of medication and potentially harming the patient.

The removal of concentrated potassium chloride from hospital inpatient units prevents administration of a fatal dose of potassium.

The ban on easily confused abbreviations and look-alike or sound-alike medications prevents serious medication errors.

When possible, a process should be mistake proofed. The more potentially harmful an error in the process could be, the more effort should be put into mistake proofing. As with the oxygen connection and the intravenous port, creating a poka yoke can require the manufacturer to develop the poka yoke.

Oxygen Outlet   Medical Air Outlet

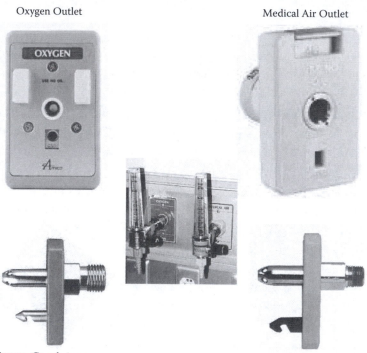

Source: Google images

FIGURE 5.14
Oxygen and medical air connections demonstrate poka yoke.

Jidoka

If there is not a way to prevent an error from occurring, the next opportunity to deal with it is to have a way to stop the process once the error has occurred. This concept is also called autonomation reflecting that it can be fulfilled by designing machinery to detect a defect and stop the process. Interestingly, an American businessman came up with such a solution before there was a concept of jidoka. At the 1854 World's Fair, Elisha Otis amazed the crowd when he ordered the only rope holding an elevator platform that he was standing on to be cut. Everyone expected disaster, but the platform fell only a few inches because Otis' elevator brake stopped the fall (Kulling, 2012). The concept of jidoka emerged in Toyota before Toyota was making cars. In 1890 Sakichi Toyoda invented a wooden loom that automatically stopped when a thread broke (Womack and Jones, 2003).

Andon

Andon is a tool to prevent passing on defects to the next step in a process by having a signal for an emerging problem. It's a Japanese term, meaning lantern or, in practice, an operational signal. In essence, andons exist when there is not poka yoke or a jidoka. In Toyota plants and manufacturing plants that have adopted Lean, there is a visual signal: a light that comes on, often accompanied by an auditory signal. The intent of the signal is to reflect the state of flow. A green light on the assembly line means all is well; flow is occurring as it should. A yellow light indicates that a worker sees something wrong and he is fixing it. A red light indicates that the worker saw something that required the line to be stopped in order not to let the defective item flow to the next step and to signal the need for help with team intervention (Chalice, 2007). This is the point when the team, including managers, helps solve the problem. Stopping a process without creating a real-time solution would be an ineffective approach and wreak havoc with production. Any worker can and should be able to pull an andon. The author of the manual at the Toyota plant in California put it in the context of respect for the worker, "It is not the conveyor that operates the men; it is the men that operate the conveyor" (Chalice, 2007). What is a more powerful endorsement of workers than telling everyone, "We trust that you know your job; you know when there is a problem that needs a solution; and you know when you need help to find that solution."

Although this tool is in the worker's hands, it needs to be emphasized that meaningful use of andons requires readiness and commitment for the worker's team as well as the appropriate level of leadership to come to the worker to create real-time solutions when needed.

We have begun to see andon-type interventions in healthcare in the use of rapid response teams, SWAT teams for emergency department divert, and stopping a procedure if an issue is identified in a timeout. All of these have been effectively used at Denver Health. One example of our rapid response is detailed below. The concept of rapid response teams grew out of the observation that patients often have a period of deterioration that is either missed or not effectively acted upon before they experience a cardiac arrest. In essence, the defect is passed along from the inpatient unit nurse or provider to the Cor Zero team. The andon is that the nurse who sees the impending problem can call the team.

Example

Denver Health has 24/7 house staff teams and all patients have a hospitalist or house staff team assigned to them. Therefore, we created an andon-like process that used the patient's own team for the response to the andon being pulled (Moldenhauer et al., 2009). A set of physiologic parameters or changes in the parameters were identified that required that the andon be pulled. A specified fall in blood pressure or oxygenation was an example of an andon trigger. When the floor nurse pulled this andon, the team, beginning with the intern, was required to come to the bedside, examine the patient, and write a note and, as appropriate, provide an intervention (no telephone orders for two aspirin and call me later). If the intern did not come to address the problem within a specified period of time, the call escalated to the resident and ultimately could escalate to the attending physician. This fulfills the andon component of having someone arrive to help solve the problem. This process is also a good example of standard work. The results of this process are illustrated in Figure 5.15. The lack of traditional use of andon-like tools undoubtedly contributed to the slow adoption of the tool. Nonetheless, it was undoubtedly used initially for those patients who were most likely to need this intervention as reflected in the marked drop in Cor Zero events on the floors. Although the rate at which patients returned to the intensive care unit within 48 hours after having been moved to a regular unit (ICU bouncebacks) was relatively low, this also decreased (Moldenhauer et al., 2009).

We need to utilize andons and andon-like tools more widely in healthcare including making certain that the correct team respond to "red lights" to initiate and complete the problem solving in real time.

Kanban

Kanban is a tool to create order, facilitate flow, and remove the waste of inventory, hoarding, and the motion of hunting and gathering while at the same time preventing process delays because some component needed for the process has run out. Kanban is the Japanese word that means sign, sign board, or signal card. It is intended to enable a system to flow by pulling needed inventory (Marchwinski, et al., 2008; Joint Commission Resources, 2008; Simpler Business System®). Figure 5.16 illustrates the basic components in effective kanban systems. A downstream customer pulls inventory from its upstream supplier at a defined threshold using a signal sent upstream with the "what, where, when, and how many." Supplies then flow downstream to the customer. Reflecting Toyota's

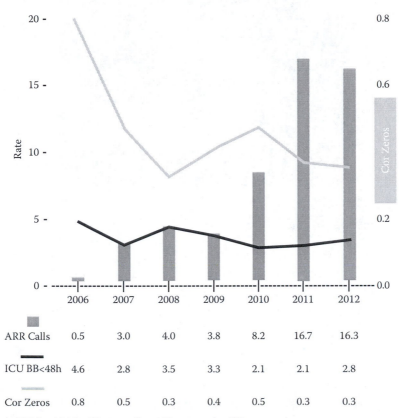

High Acuity Care*

	2006	2007	2008	2009	2010	2011	2012
ARR Calls	0.5	3.0	4.0	3.8	8.2	16.7	16.3
ICU BB<48h	4.6	2.8	3.5	3.3	2.1	2.1	2.8
Cor Zeros	0.8	0.5	0.3	0.4	0.5	0.3	0.3

* ARR Calls = Adult Rapid Response calls per 1000 acute care days ICU
BB<48h = ICU bouncebacks within 48 hours per 100 ICU transfers
Cor Zeros = Non-ICU Cor Zeros per 1000 non-ICU census days

FIGURE 5.15

Rapid response team outcomes.

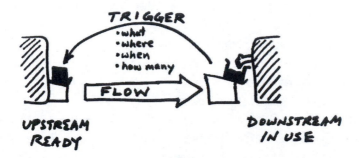

FIGURE 5.16

Well-designed kanban.

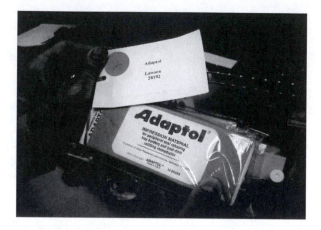

FIGURE 5.17
Kanban in the dental clinic.

simplicity, the signal can be a card attached to supplies or equipment or a light that communicates that action is required upstream to deliver the right item, in the right amount, at the right time in order to keep the system moving without waste (Joint Commission Resources, 2008).

A kanban system can be tickets on items that can be pulled when the item is used; a bin system with a couple of bins set up so when the first bin becomes empty, the second is used and the first bin is refilled; a visual or electronic system can also be used. All these types of systems have worked well at Denver Health. The ticket system shown in Figure 5.17 was utilized in the dental clinic. A ticket indicated that when the package of dental impression material with the ticket on it was removed, it was time to reorder that supply. A variety of other simple systems worked well also. Figure 5.18 shows a system using a piece of paper to indicate that it was time to reorder forms. To facilitate reordering the pertinent ordering information was printed on the colored sheet. Figure 5.19 shows how a piece of cardboard to separate bottles can be used to communicate it is time to reorder a reagent: how inexpensive is that!

A flag system shown in Figure 5.20 signals the next step for the patient in an exam room including indicating when the patient was ready for a provider. This is a variant of a kanban.

An automated kanban system is exemplified by computerized medication dispensing stations that are widely used throughout hospital units. Whatever the system, it must be accompanied by standard work to manage it or bins will sit empty.

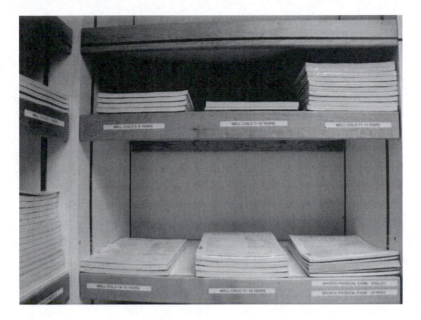

FIGURE 5.18
Kanban for the clinic form inventory.

FIGURE 5.19
Kanban in the lab.

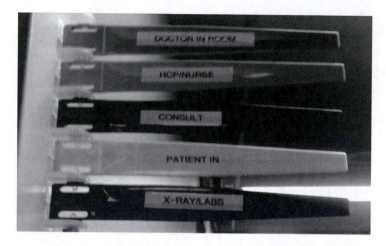

FIGURE 5.20
Clinic flag system used as a kanban.

Quick Changeover

Quick changeover is a tool aimed at the waste of waiting time and unused human talent such as surgeons waiting for the next patient in the operating room. It also facilitates increased production. The goal is quite simple: be able to limit the time and effort needed to go from the end of one process or event to the next one. A commonly used nonhealthcare example for this is pit crews at a NASCAR race (Chalice, 2007). There are many places where this concept could be used in healthcare. The operating rooms, catheterization laboratories, cleaning hospital beds, and ambulance turnarounds are settings and processes in which quick changeover would be valuable. However, there are several important differences between the healthcare teams in these situations and the NASCAR pit crew that can limit the effective use of this tool in healthcare. The pit crews have a clear signal that they need to "get at it": the car arrives. In most instances, we have not developed clear signals in healthcare to trigger a quick changeover. Does housecleaning staff really get a clear signal that a bed needs to be cleaned? Another critical difference is that the NASCAR crew knows that they need to deliver that quick changeover, fast and perfectly, or they will likely lose the race and probably be out of a job. For healthcare workers the incentives can be quite the opposite; they will get more work sooner. Despite these important differences, we had success with the quick changeover concept in bed turn-around times, operating room turnover, and ambulance turnaround times.

Examples

Using Lean tools including the quick changeover concept in cleaning vacated patients' rooms, the bed turnaround time (bed empty to bed cleaned) went from 2.58 hours to 0.73 hours. The decreased bed turnaround times mean patients may not require boarding in the emergency department, which in turn may mean that the emergency department doesn't need to go on divert, both of which affect patient access, quality, and satisfaction.

The ambulance turnaround time went from 22 minutes to 15 minutes. This change may seem small but given the number of ambulances in use in a city the size of Denver, this means 4.3 extra hours that an ambulance is on the street, which may result in decreased response time or the ability to handle more calls. Six of the A3's boxes with abbreviated text from the RIE that focused on ambulance turnaround are shown in Figure 5.21. (The A3 is the standardized format used in Lean for problem solving and communication. It is described in greater detail in the section on Tools for Structure).

Level Loading

Level loading in manufacturing is leveled production scheduling in which the mix of products and volume is scheduled to have a smoothed level of production with little variation day to day despite known/expected variation in demand (Womack and Jones, 2003). This manufacturing construct of a well-designed mix of product and volume could be used in healthcare. For example, it could be used to create the schedule for elective surgery rather than using the surgeon's preference for day and time. The concept can also take on a somewhat different construct in healthcare. The idea is simple: have the right number and types of workers and other resources to deliver value on demand without waste. In this way it eliminates the wasting of unused human talent (when you have more workers than you need) and patients waiting (when you have fewer workers than you need). In healthcare we have an abundance of information on demand by time, day, and month, but we rarely use it to create staffing. Generally, we staff by convenience and historical shift patterns. Most hospital facilities are maximally staffed Monday through Friday from 7:00 a.m. to 3:00 p.m. or 8:00 a.m. to 5:00 p.m. Some hospital departments are not even open in the evening or on weekends even though the service they provide may be needed. Rarely do we relate the staffing of one department to the flow of patients in another. For example, the housekeeping staff needed in order to do quick changeovers in beds are rarely scheduled by hospital discharge patterns or by a given unit's discharge patterns.

Box 1: Reason for Action

Streamline the processes at the beginning and end of shift in order to ensure all required tasks are completed in the allotted time.

Box 2: Current State

- Oncoming crews are expected to go in service within 15 minutes of start of shift.
- Crews were taking 22 minutes to leave the garage at start of shift.

Box 3: Target State

- Minimize distance traveled in garage by paramedics.
- Standard work is understood and completed accurately.
- Ensure that the time to complete the expected tasks does not negatively affect the 15-minute in-service goal.

Box 4: Gap Analysis

- What is/is not accomplished at the end of shift directly affects the start of shift.
- Lack of accountability.
- Variability in how ambulances are stocked.
- Certain equipment (e.g., radios, narcotics) must be controlled and scanned in/out every shift.

Box 5: Solution Approach

If:

Certain items remain on the ambulances (instead of being taken on/off).

Carts are eliminated at start of shift and ambulances are all stocked and ready to go at the start of shift.

Standard work is defined more clearly for the off-going paramedics.

Spot inspections are performed at end of shifts.

Then:

Overprocessing and motion will drastically decrease.

Crews will be able to go in-service in 15 minutes. In-service goals will be met.

Ensure oncoming crews will meet in-service goals.

Accountability will increase.

Box 6: Rapid Experiments

Experiment:

Shuffled vehicles to ensure next set of ambulances going into service is closest to supply cage.

Time crews in numerous scenarios:
- Beginning of their shift with pre-loaded ambulances (supplies and equipment).
- Ambulances not loaded but close to supply cage.

Standardized placement of equipment vehicle at end of shift.

Results:

Minimized walking but resulted in greater transportation of vehicles and time to drive them to designated bays.

Vehicles with both accurate supply levels and equipment loaded had the greatest reduction in time to service.

(Location of vehicles that were properly stocked and loaded did not make a considerable difference.)

Inconsistency between crews. Allows to verify presence of equipment; ability to assess the condition of all equipment.

FIGURE 5.21

A3 from ambulance turnaround RIE.

Example

A DH example of effective use of level loading was demonstrated by the paramedics. At first glance, one might assume that ambulance calls are completely random; however, as with most of healthcare, it is actually quite predictable if you look at the data.

For example, the area of the city with a high bar density is much busier at 2:00 a.m. on Saturday when the bars close than in a residential area. Analysis of these data enabled placing the most appropriate number of ambulances on the street at any time and establishing the most effective distribution of ambulances to meet patient demand (Robinson et al., 2012).

Level loading is a fertile area for reducing waste in healthcare.

Flow Cell

A traditional flow cell is considered to be the organization of physical space. It is a key element of the Toyota Production System (TPS) and Lean manufacturing. A flow cell organizes people, equipment, and supplies into a designed workspace, frequently U-shaped, to facilitate the flow and efficiency of work sequences (Marchwinski et al., 2008). The spatial design is complemented by clearly posted standard work for each person in the flow cell, the step before is tightly linked to the step after; the flow is transparent to all the workers, and the work is pulled by the customer demand.

In this construct the entire work sequence yields one-piece flow and avoids the wastes of overproduction, excess inventory, and waiting while preventing underproduction, which reduces revenue and creates waiting from the customer's perspective. Some Lean purists might argue that flow cells are only found in manufacturing. In truth, flow cells are a new concept in healthcare and they have had limited implementation. Most of our healthcare spaces have not been designed with one-piece flow in mind.

There is a somewhat broader definition of flow cells that goes beyond physical layout and is clearly applicable to healthcare. In this construct, one organizes the work of a common process by organizing the space using 5S, organizing the people with standard work, and achieving transparency of the workflow with visual management, all of which yields pull and one-piece flow (Simpler Business System). Using this concept, the common processes in a given VS would be organized into flow cells. For example, in the emergency department the common flows would likely include triage, fast track, and trauma. These common patient processes would represent individual flow cells that would be created with 5S, standard work, visual management, pull, and one-piece flow. These characteristics of flow cells would make their use in many healthcare processes highly desirable.

We developed several examples of flow cells, including document scanning in the health information department and patient flow in the pediatric clinic, and in emergency department fast track.

Examples

The document scanning team was organized into a flow cell. This reduced the needed FTEs from eight to four and they were reassigned to other work in the health information management section.

The pediatric clinic flow cell shown in Figure 5.22 was accomplished using the currently configured rooms but changing the linkages of work (O'Connor et al., 2010). The medical assistant (shown on the left) and the provider (shown on the right) in the flow cell worked concurrently (solid connecting line) rather than sequentially. This flow cell creation reduced the mean visit time from 31 ± 14 to 25 ± 1 minutes ($p < 0.001$) while maintaining the value-added time of the patient with the provider. This change permitted the number of visits per session to increase by 12% enabling greater patient access with the same number of providers.

Visual Management

Visual management is another tool central to Lean implementation. Each word in this concept is important: it is both about being able to see and managing what you see. The fundamental goal of visual management is to create transparency in order to make abnormalities, problems, and conditions obvious at a glance to everyone and then to drive the desired behaviors in all who are involved in the process. Visual management takes aim at virtually all wastes, enabling increased productivity, safety, and quality.

There are three common levels of visual management listed in Table 5.6. Some authors add a fourth level called visual guarantees that can equate to poka yoke (Galsworth, 1997). There can be some conceptual overlap as one begins to apply these levels of visual management. The robust underlying concept is transparent communication of what is important.

Visual indicators passively share information that an individual may use or not (Galsworth, 1997). Way-finding signs or information signs, such as the signs with a stylized picture of a man or a woman to mark the type of restroom, are common examples of this first level of visual management. Another example is the white and black railroad crossing sign that is before the railroad track. On most urban healthcare campuses the way-finding types of visual management leave much to be desired.

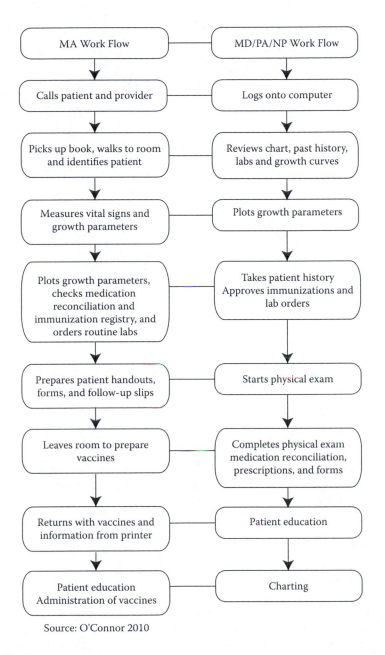

Source: O'Connor 2010

FIGURE 5.22
Pediatric clinic flow cell. (MA: medical assistant, MD: doctor, PA: physician assistant, NP: nurse practitioner.)

TABLE 5.6

Types of Visual Management

Visual Indicator

Signs with information
    Black and white railroad crossing sign
    Male or female figure on restroom door

Visual Signal

Signs to gain attention and elicit certain action
    Red traffic light
    Nurse call light

Visual Controls

Signs intended to enforce behavior
    Railroad crossing barrier
    Operating suite sterile corridor marking

Visual Guarantees

Railroad crossing overpass
Badge entry for maternity ward

Visual signals actively gain our attention, deliver a message of a changed condition, and are intended to elicit appropriate action (Galsworth, 1997). An everyday example is a red light sending the message, "Don't go through this intersection." Another common example is the flashing red lights before the track as the train is approaching (the train also blows its horn, an auditory signal). Healthcare examples of visual signals are nurse call lights, cardiac and vital sign monitors, head of bed monitors, and bed tracking systems with divert messages.

Example

One innovative visual signal shown in Figure 5.23 was part 5S and part standard work. It is a multicolored, multimessage flipchart on the door of a patient's room on the inpatient units. Prior to the development of the flipchart, different pieces of paper with various messages related to care of the patient would be pinned on the door of the patient's room. Because this approach had no standard work, critically important information could be missed, potentially causing patient harm. One nursing unit developed the flipchart and tested it. It was then produced and used on all units, demonstrating the Lean process of spread.

FIGURE 5.23
Flipchart for door of patient room.

Visual controls attempt to actually enforce actions or behavior, although they can still be ignored, albeit with serious consequences. A visual control example is the gate that lowers as a barrier to crossing the track when the approaching train trips an automatic switch. In healthcare sterile corridor entrances in the operating room suite or warnings with barriers in the MRI areas are visual controls.

Visual guarantees usually have a structural element that in essence creates a poka yoke (Galsworth, 1997). If the track had a visual guarantee or poka yoke, it would be something like a bridge or overpass for cars to travel over the train tracks. One example of a visual guarantee is the restricted entry that many hospitals have put in place in their maternity area that requires specific badges or actual checking of people before permitting entry.

These levels of visual management represent a hierarchy that is well exemplified in the management of railroad crossings: the visual indicator of the crossing sign, the visual signal of the flashing red lights, the visual control of the lowered gate, and the possible visual guarantee of an overpass. Combining the hierarchy of visual management tools provides greater safety than any one of the tools would have alone. In healthcare we use hierarchical visual management in MRI areas (Kanal et al., 2002). 5S is the most foundational of all visual management tools and it must be in place in any Lean organization (see Tools to Eliminate Waste section). Kanban systems and andons are also visual management tools. We used visual management at the organizational, VS, and workplace level at Denver Health.

Production Boards

A type of visual management tool utilizes transparent communication to facilitate process flow. A production control board is an example of this visual tool. Its function is to assist in problem identification and problem solving. A production board is posted in the work area and provides metrics of the area's operations so that supervisors, frontline staff, and even visitors will know the status of operations at a glance, in real time. Production control boards display agreed-upon measures of flow that can be reviewed frequently, sometimes hourly. Generally, the more real time the measures are, the more helpful. Overall, a production board must be used to manage the workflow. If it is not used in this way, it is a wasted effort. A very simple production monitoring board in a manufacturing process would show the needed production per time (widgets per hour) and the current production rate. A well-designed production board is not only a tool for managers and supervisors. It should be readily visible to the workers so they would know if they are keeping pace. In fact, a well-designed production board benefits the people using it to achieve relentless improvement.

In implementing this type of visual management in your institution several guidelines may be helpful:

- Pictures instead of text can be helpful in displaying standard work.
- Charts and signs should be simple and visible by the workers from their worksites.
- The metrics being displayed on the chart should reflect an agreed-upon standard of performance.
- The information displayed should be directed toward the team, not individuals.
- The information displayed should facilitate problem solving.
- The team should have an agreed-upon method to address departures from the standard on the chart.

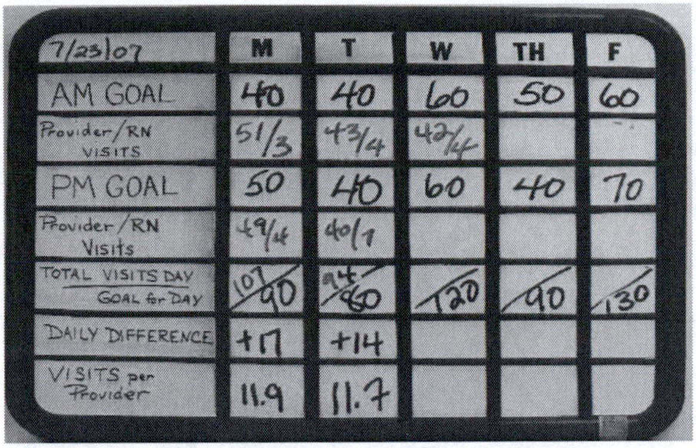

FIGURE 5.24

Peds/teen clinic visits per session production board.

Examples

A production control board shown in Figure 5.24 improved throughput in primary care clinics. It was a simple whiteboard to track productivity on a daily basis and the team used it in daily huddles. Monday and Tuesday work has occurred and overall daily production was ahead of target for those days.

A production control board used in an outpatient clinic to post wait times is shown in Figure 5.25. It notifies the entire work team and the waiting patients which provider is on time, which provider is 15 minutes behind, and which provider is 30 minutes or more behind schedule. Staffing is adjusted by pulling appropriate resources to assist providers that are either in the yellow or red zones.

A production control board shown in Figure 5.26 addressed the turnover times of operating rooms used for ophthalmology procedures. Baseline data documented room turnover between cataract repair cases in excess of 20 minutes. The agreed upon room turnover time for a routine cataract case was eight minutes. The visual management tool was implemented by the team to monitor the actual room turnover times. This allowed the team to manage performance against the standard and to problem solve as a team in real time as well as to assess if certain staff were often outside the target.

Production Control Boards are also useful at the VS level. Figure 5.27 illustrates that these boards are more complex but serve the same purpose of monitoring the performance and flow of the VS.

TOOLS FOR QUALITY

Lean's focus on delivering value, reducing waste from the customer/patient's perspective, and eliminating defects underscores Lean's attention

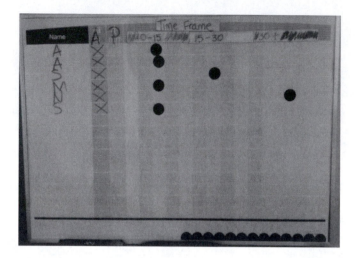

FIGURE 5.25
Clinic wait time by provider.

	Case 1	Case 2	Case 3	Case 4	Case 5	Case 6	Case 7
Monday	⬤	⬤	⬤	⬤	⬤	⬤	⬤
Tuesday	⬤	⬤	⬤	⬤	⬤	⬤	⬤
Wednesday	⬤	⬤	⬤	⬤	⬤	⬤	⬤
Thursday	⬤	⬤	⬤	⬤	⬤	⬤	⬤
Friday	⬤	⬤	⬤	⬤	⬤	⬤	⬤

⬤ Room Ready ≤ 8 mins.   ⬤ Room Ready > 8 mins.

FIGURE 5.26
Opthalomology production control board for OR turnover times.

to quality. Therefore, many of the tools to reduce waste that have been discussed are also tools for improving quality. These multipurpose tools include standard work, poka yoke, jidoka, andon, and visual management. The role of level loading by managing both elective procedures and surges has been proposed as an important quality and safety tool (Litvak and Fineberg, 2013). Some authors would include the 5 whys as a quality tool inasmuch as it focuses on getting to the root cause of problems

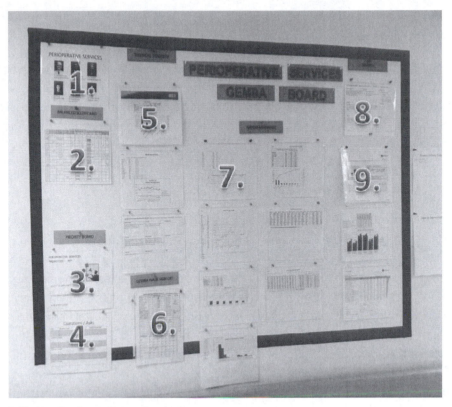

1. Photos of perioperative services leaders
2. Balanced scorecard
3. Priority board listing top three priorities
4. Questions and "asks"
5. Financial metrics
6. Gemba walk sign-off sheet
7. Patient experience metrics
8. A3 for tactics addressing issues
9. Growth metrics

FIGURE 5.27
Perioperative services vs. production control board.

(Koenigsaecker, 2013). Not surprisingly, there is also a specific Lean tool for quality management, appropriately dubbed quality checks, that include self-checks and successive checks (Koenigsaecker, 2013). Everyone should check her own work before sending it on (self-check) and there should be a system for an employee to perform a check on a sample of the work which is being passed to him (successive checks). Healthcare examples of successive checks are two patient identifiers that are used for a variety of procedures, the checks for administering blood products and timeouts for procedures.

TOOLS FOR STRUCTURE

The TPOC, identifications of VSs and VS maps described above as tools for prioritization and alignment, are also tools that create structure for the Lean journey. Two other important tools that provide structure for the Lean efforts are RIEs and the A3 method of problem solving and communication.

Rapid Improvement Events

Liker has observed that RIEs (also called kaizen workshops) are a "remarkable social invention" (Liker, 2004). In a similar vein, Koenigsaecker (2013) has said that the RIE is "the most effective, perhaps the only way ... to achieve financial results, [create] opportunities to learn and change culture." The RIE is a radical invention/intervention for most healthcare entities in terms of participants, pace, standardization, and approval process. Generally, in healthcare institutions when a problem is identified, a committee is formed. It has been said that "Committees waste hours and save the 'minutes.'" How true! Committees grow in size in proportion to the scope or complexity of the problem, operationalizing the belief that every possible stakeholder needs to be at the table. Moreover, often any of these stakeholders has veto power over a potential solution. The committee often meets at variable intervals with varying participants present. Although we know when committees begin, they often do not have a hard stop. They are anything but rapid. Months may elapse without a clear definition of the problem, let alone a clear, implemented, and monitored solution. Committees are frequently loosely structured in terms of process. A committee report usually requires approval and action by those in leadership who initiated the committee.

RIEs are in marked contrast to all these committee characteristics. All three words in "rapid improvement event" are important, central to Lean, and organizationally radical. "Rapid" refers to the fact that waste is identified, removed, and a new and improved process established and implemented in four days. This is breathtakingly fast for a non-Lean organization. "Improvement" means there is an actual solution to the problem that removes waste and that the solution is implemented and the metrics to verify and monitor the improvement are established. "Event" conveys a self-contained, time-limited process. The RIE follows standard work regarding the tasks that are done and the days on which specific tasks are performed. This is detailed in Chapter 7. An RIE includes six to ten people, usually including frontline people, rather than traditional leadership appointed to a committee. RIE participants are not all from the area of focus. There is no voting, so there are no vetoes.

One Denver Health RIE rule was, "No New Resources," which rarely is a committee rule. There are three other aspects in which RIEs differ markedly from committees. What the team decides to do is done (unless the process conflicts with or violates some compliance or regulatory mandate). There is no approval process through a chain of command. In fact, the new process is often in place at the end of the RIE week or very soon thereafter. This is real employee respect and empowerment; it turns traditional hierarchy on its head and the leadership must be prepared for this. This is not to say the leadership no longer leads. In fact, in the application of Lean, leadership sets strategy, system metrics, and priorities through the establishment of the True North, the TPOC, and the VSs (see Tools to Create Prioritization and Alignment section). The executive team operationalizes this through the VS metrics and the identification of RIEs. Thus, in Lean, leaders lead and the frontline employees solve the daily work problems—a perfect division of labor.

RIEs are a must activity in any organization on a Lean journey. They are the primary Lean vehicle to drive organizational cultural change. Without RIEs, organizations revert to a project mentality that does not provide the pace or the employee involvement for organizational transformation. The role of RIEs in Denver Health's Lean journey is described in detail in Chapter 7.

A3

The A3 is an amazing power tool enabling both structured problem solving and structured, succinct, clear communication. It creates a common approach to problem solving and a common language across an organization. So what is this magic power tool—it must be some new computer "app"—right?—wrong. The A3 refers to the least sophisticated thing you could imagine in today's world: a standard international-sized piece of paper which is approximately 11 × 17 inches in the United States (Joint Commission Resources, 2008). The size is not as critical as are the boxes that compose an A3, which lead you through a standard method of problem solving and a standard manner to describe each component (OK, yes,

TABLE 5.7

A3 Structure

First "pre box." List of participants in process
Second "pre box." If an RIE, a VS map picture and position of RIE in the
    VS

Box 1 Reason for Action

Box 2 Current State

Box 3 Target State

Box 4 Gap Analysis

Box 5 Solution Approach

Box 6 Rapid Experiments

Box 7 Completion Plan

Box 8 Confirmed State

Box 9 Insights

---

you can put it on a computer). There are a number of different versions of the A3 boxes (Chalice, 2007; Shook, 2008; Jimmerson, 2007; Hafer, 2012). Some sensei use pictures as well as words in the boxes to resonate with both left-brain and right-brain thinkers. Whatever the specific boxes or depictions, the A3 essentially represents the same sequence of thinking and communicating. The A3 needs to be factual and easy to understand. The A3 should flow like a perfect abstract in a grant application or a presentation at a scientific meeting.

Denver Health used the nine boxes listed in Table 5.7 that were from our Simpler sensei. There are two "pre boxes" before the nine established A3 boxes that we found helpful additions. We used the A3 format for RIE report outs. In that setting each box, often including the two "pre boxes," was a slide.

The first pre box should contain the following information: the VS from which RIE came, the executive staff sponsor, the facilitator from the Lean systems improvement department, the team lead, the process owner, and the team members. A picture of the team is a nice touch. The second pre box can be a picture of the VS map with a notation of where this RIE falls in the VS. Although 90% of RIEs should be part of a VS, we did occasionally allow stand-alone RIEs, but this should be limited in order to avoid the "drive-by RIE" approach, which does not maximize flow of a specific process.

Box 1 Reason for Action: This is a clear problem statement with the aim and scope to be considered in addressing the problem. Some call this the burning platform or to go to medical analogy, the chief complaint.

Box 2 Current State (also called Initial State): This should be a qualitative and quantitative description of what you have actually observed and measured. This is a data-rich description; often it will contain graphic data. If this box doesn't have hard data on the current state for the process you are intending to change, the event will likely not be useful. Lack of hard data reflects a lack of careful observation and planning.

Box 3 Target State: This should be an equally qualitative and quantitative description of what the new process will be when you have removed the targeted waste. It should reflect the same information categories that are in Box 2 and have the same graphic data. This target state should represent significant improvement over the current state. Small improvements are not worth the time and effort for an RIE. In order to avoid "softball" RIEs, we set a minimum financial benefit target of $50,000 per RIE. We did not always achieve this, however, we found the target helpful. Although 90% of all RIEs should have such a clear financial metric, we did allow a few events that were called foundational. These RIEs focused on a key process that was necessary as a structural basis for future events. During the presentation at report out it was noted that this was such an event. This can be a slippery slope so if you do foundational RIEs, enforce the rareness.

Box 4 Gap Analysis: This is a description of the barriers that are preventing you from going from the current state to the desired target state. To fill in this box you will need to use a number of the Lean tools such as the 5 whys or the fishbone to identify the root causes for the barriers. The actual fishbone can be included in the box. Teams can construct a slide of the gap analysis with the five columns: current state, target state, gap, problem statement, and root cause.

Box 5 Solution Approach: This box describes specific solutions that will address the barriers/root causes detailed in Box 4. The solution should use Lean methods. The slide can be set up with two columns: If and Then. At this point these are potential solutions (If) awaiting rapid experiments for confirmation of feasibility and expected outcomes (Then). Therefore, the solutions need to be sufficiently specific and detailed so they can actually be tested by rapid experiments.

Box 6 Rapid Experiments: In this box, the rapid experiments that were performed to confirm feasibility and desired outcome are described. It must be emphasized that these are rapid experiments done during rapid improvement events. They are not long controlled studies. The slide should include the actual experiment description, the expected outcome, and the actual outcome. In the spirit of Plan, Do, Study, Act (PDSA), if the rapid experiment doesn't yield the expected result, the team needs to initiate other experiments.

Box 7 Completion Plan: This box can list all the process changes that were implemented during an RIE week. Any actions still pending should be very few in an RIE week. You must be vigilant about RIEs slipping into project or committee modes. Usually, the only items that should be awaiting completion in RIE should be some communication, some training, and schedule changes for areas where schedules have already been distributed two or three months in advance and perhaps, an HIT augmentation. A caution is needed regarding HIT; you must avoid teams falling into the trap of an HIT solution to all barriers. We solved this in part with our "No New Resources" rule. Listed items can include "Just Do Its" that have been done in the RIE week (teams like to show all they have accomplished). When an A3 is used in a TPOC, the completion list can be long. Any item in the completion plan needs to be specific with the name of the responsible person and date for completion. The completion plan for an RIE must be reviewed at the 30-, 60-, and 90-day follow-up meetings.

Box 8 Confirmed State: This box relates back to the target state and should detail the specific metrics to be used, the frequency with which they will be measured, and the visual management to be utilized. The metrics should include the baseline data and the target state metrics.

Box 9 Insights: This box contains the insights from the team. These can be gathered at the end of each day or at the end of the last day of an RIE, VSM, or TPOC. These insights can relate to the organization, the process that was examined, the Lean activity, or the group interactions. Some find it useful to divide the insights into aspects that were positive and aspects that could be improved.

Although this may seem like a lot of material, remember in the Toyota world this was on an approximately 11 × 17-inch sheet of paper. It needs to be concise; it is your abstract, not the published paper!

A3s enable the entire organization to speak one language. At Denver Health, the A3 became the platform for problem solving and communication at the enterprise, VS, and worksite levels. Budget and personnel requests were submitted as A3s.

TOOLS FOR DESIGN

Toyota and Lean gurus have developed a set of tools and approaches for designing new space and for developing new products (Hino, 2002; Koenigsaecker, 2013). Although there has been limited healthcare application to date of these tools, there are undoubtedly uses for both of these types of tools in healthcare. In the past new healthcare space was designed by committee and rarely focused on delivering flow without barriers and often accommodated wastes (think waiting rooms). As we enter an era of health reform, all successful healthcare providers will be designing new approaches to healthcare delivery and tools for new product development will be useful as these organizations strive for innovation. In both designing new space and new products or approaches, the other Lean tools need to be used. Any new space or new product should be as waste-free as possible.

3P and 2P

There are two tools we found particularly helpful in constructing space or in occupying already constructed space with a new activity. These were 3P and 2P, respectively. As we have seen many times, there is simplicity in Lean tools and in their names. The 3P is named for the three components beginning with P: production, preparation, and process. As I am sure you can guess, 2P is for process and preparation. In manufacturing 3P is commonly used in product development. Its use, in one industry in new machine design, produced outcomes at one quarter the capital cost of other non-Lean methodologies (Koenigsaecker, 2013). The 3P and 2P processes are much like an RIE format. However, these processes differ from RIEs in that the teams are larger, they focus heavily on the flows of people and supplies, and the event format is designed to examine seven different alternatives: a design version of 5 whys or the 5 hows. The use of seven alternatives prevents teams from coming to closure too quickly on a particular alternative just as the 5 whys keep teams from mistaking the symptom for the root cause.

Vertical Value Stream

Another design tool is a vertical VS (Simpler Business System). It was used by Denver Health as a project design and project management tool. A vertical VS shares some characteristics with a traditional horizontal VS mapping. These are four- to five-day events with an executive sponsor, a facilitator, and team lead. The intent is to develop the least waste way to deliver a new product or service. Some specific wastes targeted by vertical VSs are missed deadlines, rework, scheduling conflicts, and importantly, the overproduction and misused human talent that happens when too many people or the wrong people participate in numerous planning meetings. There are some important differences from traditional VSs. At Denver Health, a VS and its RIEs have a rule of "No New Resources." Obviously, many new products or services require new resources. Traditional VS mappings have teams of six to eight, whereas vertical VSs have 10 to 15 team members, reflecting the complexity of projects and new process design over improving an existing process. Many VSs such as perioperative service, revenue cycle, and others are expected to generate many RIEs over a multiyear period. In contrast, a vertical VS is a time-limited planning event. It can be a single event. Vertical VSs have gates or freeze points, at which points all steps are required to be completed within a specified time frame to move to the next gate. These are often go/no go decision points. Once a gate is reached, there is no going back. We found a seasoned sensei necessary for the conduct of this more complex tool.

6

Structure for Lean Implementation

SENSEI GUIDANCE

Sensei is a Japanese term that refers to a teacher with a mastery of the discipline. Think of a sensei as a seasoned attending for the Lean discipline, a person with deep and broad knowledge and deep personal experience. Some have interpreted the term to mean, "One who has traveled the path before." This clearly is not the old house staff model of "See one, do one, teach one."

As with any discipline, we learn from our teachers and the more gifted and experienced the teachers are, the more we can learn. Our teachers give us foundational knowledge and they oversee our practice. Lean is no different. Both the information transfer and the oversight are important. Despite our enthusiasm for this book, other authors on Lean have stated, "A book is not a sensei" (Brenner and McKibben, 2011). Given this perspective, a question that leadership needs to ask early in the Lean journey is, "Do we need an outside person or group with extensive Lean knowledge and experience to be our sensei and to guide our organization on our Lean transformation?"

We answered "Yes" to that question as have other Lean pioneers in healthcare such as Virginia Mason Hospital and Medical Center, ThedaCare, and Park Nicollet Health Services. Our consulting group's knowledge and experience as well as their externality gave them the ability to provide meaningful guidance and constructive criticism, and to push us in ways that might have been difficult for an internal person. Although this may change over time as healthcare institutions adopt Lean, few in healthcare now have had deep and long experience in leading Lean transformation in their own organization to serve as a sensei. Therefore, currently most

TABLE 6.1

Characteristics to Consider in Choosing a Sensei or Lean Consultants

Sensei who have held senior leadership position
Sensei who have led Lean transformation at an enterprise level
Sensei who have conducted over 100 rapid improvement events
Sensei who are excellent teachers in one-on-one coaching and mentoring, in small groups, and in the classroom setting
Sensei who can work in a healthcare environment (ideally have healthcare experience)
Sensei who can cultivate trust and relationships at all levels from the executive team to the frontline staff
Consultants who utilize sensei with these characteristics
Consultants who focus on Lean as a transformational journey, not just on the Lean tools

sensei have had their deep immersion in Lean through leading manufacturing companies on their Lean transformation. We consider several characteristics that are detailed in Table 6.1 worth considering in choosing a Lean consultant group.

It is useful to know how many RIEs the sensei has actually conducted. Those with decades of experience have said that after personally participating in 12 events you have only completed kindergarten and after 100 events you become a convert to Lean; you may not yet be a sensei (Koenigsaecker, 2013)! This is similar to the concept that it takes 10 years in the practice of a medical discipline to become a master clinician. Our sensei's role and time commitment evolved as we became more experienced with Lean, much as the role of a seasoned attending is different for a medical student than for a fellow or a junior faculty member. The sensei's initial primary duties were to teach our executives, facilitators, and our Black Belts about the journey, the philosophical underpinnings, and the tools in the Lean tool box, and to oversee the conduct of the TPOC, VSAs, and RIEs. The sensei's role evolved into directing the disciplined delivery; rigorous and consistent use of key Lean tools such as flow cells, takt time, and visual management; driving the pace; directing the use of the more advanced Lean efforts such as 3Ps; and more intense teaching of the executive team and the individuals in the Lean systems improvement department. Initially, our external sensei was only present for the two RIE weeks/month. This proved to be a limitation for our learning and our pace; therefore, we moved to a weekly presence.

MANAGEMENT STRUCTURE

Given that every healthcare organization has its own organizational structure, the governance and oversight of the Lean transformation will vary, with reporting often being to the chief operating officer, the chief medical officer, or the chief quality officer. However, we believe that the Lean effort should report to the chief executive officer as nothing is more important to the organization than its culture, quality, cost, and human development: all parts of Lean transformation.

Within six months of starting the Lean journey, we realized that the preparation, conduct, and follow-up of RIEs and the pace of Lean activity required a group of people trained in and dedicated to the Lean transformation. A Lean systems improvement department was created. We chose as the director a respected individual who had many years of clinical and administrative experience in the organization, rising from the ranks of a respiratory therapist to the administrative director of the department of medicine, rather than someone from the outside trained in system engineering or Lean.

Initially, as we were exploring our path for transformation we hired an engineer for process mapping. Subsequently, we hired six more facilitators, two of whom were engineers, one of whom had direct manufacturing experience; four were recruited internally. Key components of the facilitator job description are detailed in Table 6.2. These were not new positions but rather positions that were reclaimed from some of the initial work in the revenue cycle. Their primary responsibilities related to the management of the RIEs for two VSs, supporting the VS steering committees and process owners with organizational issues including following metrics, and assisting in training the Black Belts. Seven years into our Lean journey, a career ladder was created with the establishment of the position of senior facilitator, which reflected a greater level of documented Lean experience and knowledge. The training of facilitators is detailed in the Training section of Chapter 7. The Lean initiative, the consulting sensei, and the director of the Lean systems improvement department reported to the CEO.

The executive staff fulfills a critical role in Lean implementation, participating in a variety of ways. The entire executive staff participated in the

TABLE 6.2

Essentials of Job Description for Lean Facilitator

Education

Bachelor's degree in healthcare administration, industrial engineering, or related field

Experience

Two years' experience with Lean initiatives. Healthcare management experience preferred

Knowledge and Skills

Knowledge of Lean/Toyota production systems
Ability to use computer tools
Basic statistical analysis and data management skills
Strong verbal and written communication skills
Strong interpersonal and leadership skills
Strong organizational skills

Job Duties

Coordinates planning, execution, and follow up for rapid improvement events for two
  value streams
Functions as facilitator for rapid improvement events
Teaches and coaches individuals and teams in Lean principles, tools, and management

Supervision

Reports to director of Lean systems improvement department

TPOC exercise, establishing the VSs for the year. Each VS was overseen by an executive staff member who became the VS sponsor. For example, the chief financial officer was the executive sponsor for the revenue cycle VS, the COO was the executive sponsor for the behavioral health VS, the director of community health services was the sponsor for that VS, and the chief human resources officer was the sponsor for the human resource VS. The duties of the executive staff including their specific roles as executive sponsors of VSs are detailed in Table 6.3. Some would dub this leadership standard work. At initial blush this may seem like added work, but these activities can and should replace other activities and should provide deeper knowledge of the operations than the older standard approaches to work did.

The CEO, the executive staff sponsors, their assigned facilitators, the director of the Lean systems department, and consulting sensei met monthly to review the past and future RIEs and other activities. A VS steering committee was composed of the executive staff member, the facilitator for the VS, and the VS owner who generally was the person responsible

TABLE 6.3

Duties of Executive Staff Members

Duties in Lean Leadership

Participate in the TPOC exercise

Participate in two RIEs per year (not necessarily in their VS)

Visit value stream and other areas of responsibility work areas (*gemba* walks)
  regularly reviewing 5S status, standard work, production boards

Monitor the activities of the Black Belts in their areas

Duties of Value Stream Sponsor

Form VS steering committee

Participate in the mapping of the VS including establishing RIEs for year

Coordinate establishment of VS metrics

Hold monthly VS steering committee meetings

Deliver RIE kickoff training

Oversee pre-work for upcoming RIEs

Attend end-of-day debrief of RIEs in VS

Attend all RIE report out events

for the operations of the area. All steering committees that had a clinical component either had a physician as the executive sponsor or included a physician leader as a steering committee member. The financial analyst assigned to the area was also a member of the steering committee.

A critical responsibility of the steering committee was to keep the pace of eight to ten RIEs per year. Although this was the goal, it was not easy to achieve this pace. Some VSs were more successful at this than others. Sizing the RIEs can be challenging especially in the beginning when you tend to either overestimate or underestimate how much a team can do in four full days. Examples of RIEs in some VSs are shown in Table 6.4.

The steering committee's monthly meeting followed standard work (Appendix Figure A.1) that included confirming the VS was on target to meet metrics, reviewing the previous three RIEs to see they are on target for metrics and any completion plan, reviewing planning for the next three RIEs, and establishing team members, metrics, and ROI.

Another component of the implementation structure was a dedicated group to document and review the metrics for all VSs, RIEs, and Black Belts. This group was composed of the director of the Lean systems improvement department, the associate CFO, and the CEO. This group met monthly. The details of the metrics and their management are discussed in the metrics section of Chapter 8.

TABLE 6.4

Examples of Rapid Improvement: Events in Value Streams

Community Health Services (Ambulatory Primary Care Clinics)

Provider Flow Cell: Pediatrics
Registration Flow Cell
Medication Reconciliation

Perioperative Services

Preoperative Clinic Standard Work
Chair Side Registration
SCOR Packet Content and Flow

Obstetrics and Gynecology

Obstetrics Admission Process
Mom/Baby Discharge Process
NICU Discharge Process

Behavioral Health

Admission Standard Work
Plan of Care Flow Cell
Discharge Pharmacy Process

Revenue Cycle

Electronic Facility Billing
Medicaid Pending Claims
One-Stop Coding Edits

7

Deploying Lean

TRAINING

How, what, and when to train are always questions at the start of a new initiative. One approach is to make sure every employee is trained in the new initiative at the start of the journey. This is expensive and training that is not used soon is often forgotten. Another approach is extensive training of the leaders. Virginia Mason, an early adopter of Lean, sends its leaders to Japan to immerse them in the actual doing of Lean (Kenny, 2011). Although this undoubtedly is beneficial, it, too, is expensive and would be politically and financially infeasible for many institutions. This would not have been possible at Denver Health. Thus, we opted for basic training of the leadership, more extensive training of a small group of selected managers (Black Belts) and the Lean facilitators onsite, and just-in-time training of the workforce as they participated in various Lean events. The executive staff and the physician directors of service (departmental chairs) received four hours of "Lean 101." As in any discipline, Lean has a body of knowledge that must be acquired; therefore, in retrospect, more intensive training of this group in the beginning would have been helpful. This leadership group read a number of well-established books on Lean for our joint journal club, including *Lean Thinking* by Womack and Jones (2003).

A handpicked group of 25 departmental administrators and mid-managers who were respected individuals, eager learners, early adopters, and doers were picked to become our first cadre of Black Belts. This initial group was given 48 hours of Lean training by a local external manufacturing consulting group. Over the ensuing years, we perfected our own training and conducted Black Belt training twice a year for a cadre of 25–30 individuals who were recommended by the executive staff. Our internal group also trained any new facilitators and provided formal training to others outside our institution through the Lean Academy we had established in response to numerous requests. The areas covered in Black Belt training are detailed in Table 7.1.

Each workshop except the last day was a full day. The workshop training series was distributed over approximately six weeks to have minimal impact on clinical duties. In addition, over the years our sensei conducted regular and more in-depth training for our executives, facilitators, and Black Belts. At the beginning of our Lean journey all mid-managers were given two hours of general Lean training and two hours of training in 5S.

All RIE weeks began with one hour of training. This "just-in-time" training consisted of a 15-minute introduction by one of the executive staff sponsors emphasizing the importance of Lean to Denver Health's mission and of the work that was to be done during the week. The facilitators then presented an overview of the Lean principles, the eight wastes and 5S. The group then engaged in a Lean exercise that demonstrated a basic Lean tool such as a scavenger hunt to underscore the role of 5S. They started the actual RIE with the waste walk. During the RIE week the members of the team were exposed to a wide array of Lean tools. This provided just-in-time training for employees.

BLACK BELTS

The concept of Denver Health Lean Black Belts evolved over the first year of our Lean journey. Any CEO who has been around for a long time can name the individuals in the organization who can embrace and lead change. These individuals can be the leaven for institutional transformation because they are often at the critical interface between senior leadership and the frontline employees. We took the classical Six Sigma term (now also used in Lean), which seemed to capture a Japanese image of karate-chopping waste, and dubbed these individuals Black Belts.

The first 25 Black Belts were individuals who were not "turned off" by manufacturing language and examples and were creative enough to see the applicability in healthcare. As we continued our Lean journey, we had many healthcare examples and the individual's ability to translate from manufacturing to healthcare became less relevant.

The first group of Black Belts was initially asked to identify, complete, and report a project in six months using Lean. Midway through the

TABLE 7.1

Black Belt Training

Workshop 1

History of Lean
Lean at Denver Health
Lean principles
Go to a work site; Lean principles in action
Introduction to A3
Standard work discussion and activity

Workshop 2

Process map, spaghetti diagram, communication circle, waste walk, time observations
Takt time calculations
Go to work site for waste walk
Transformation plan of care
Value stream analysis
Quality function deployment
Rapid improvement events

Workshop 3

Visual management
Go to work site for visual management
5S
Go to a work site to do 5S
Production boards
Poka yoke
Kanban
Level loading

Workshop 4

Watch toast-making video
Quick changeover
Root cause analysis
Presentations by Black Belts of representative BB efforts
Expectations for Black Belts
Black Belt ideas and share point site
Metrics
Servant leadership

Workshop 5

Flow cells
Exercise to integrate all of learning

Workshop 6 (1/2 day)

Testing Lean knowledge

---

six-month period, it became clear that this slow pace would not be transformative, would not fulfill the Lean objective of continuous improvement, and would seem to be an "add-on" to their current work, rather than a new way of doing work. Therefore, going forward, Black Belts were asked to use Lean in their day-to-day work and to report monthly (later quarterly) in a standardized format their use of Lean to reduce waste in their area (Appendix Figure A.2). One Black Belt noted, "You only need to look in your trash can to see some obvious waste you could remove." For the first four years, all the reports were read by me and were often returned with comments (in Denver Health speak, "Love Notes from Patty"). This served to underscore the importance of this effort and provide some guidance and direction. It also provided me with a broad view of the enterprise.

Over time the organization had trained over 300 Black Belts, the majority of whom were in leadership positions. All new mid-managers, all new physician directors of service, and any new executive staff member were expected to be trained as Black Belts. By year seven there were 257 active Black Belts including 52 physicians and 59 nurse leaders.

Beginning in year four, the Black Belts were each asked to achieve a target of $30,000 of financial benefit/year. Their formalized reports were vetted by the associate CFO before the financial benefit was finalized. In addition to the reports and the financial expectations, each Black Belt was expected to participate in at least two RIEs per year, often functioning as the team lead. The latter expectation turned out to be an issue, although not for the reason you might think. Because the Black Belts were quite knowledgeable both about Lean and management they were asked to lead many teams, too many. Therefore, we had to ask the executive staff sponsors to avoid the overuse of the Black Belts in this way. The Black Belts met as a group quarterly with the CEO, the director of the Lean systems improvement department, the associate CFO, and often the sensei. These meetings provided Lean education, highlighted Black Belt achievements, and provided feedback to the Lean leadership team and the CEO.

Information on participation and achievement of these expectations by individual Black Belts was given to their executive staff. Excellence in this role was a strong consideration for institutional advancement. The training, the doing of Lean, the reports, and the meetings served to provide this group with new skills. Moreover, through the training and in the BB meetings, the Black Belts had opportunities to work together with counterparts in other parts of the organization, breaking down silos. Thus, this effort was in line with Toyota's philosophy of building people. Moreover, their efforts had significant financial and quality results. Multiple examples are provided to underscore the power of this "Lean Army" in an organization.

Example

One joint effort was by a Black Belt from respiratory therapy and a Black Belt from pharmacy. This is a great example of the collaboration that can occur by having a cadre of Black Belts who might not have ever interacted in our old models of problem identification and problem solving. Patients with reactive airway disease who are admitted to the hospital are treated with inhaler therapy. These inhalers are designed for multiple doses (managing for daily improvement [MDIs]), and usually contain about a month's supply of doses, suggesting they would certainly last almost any patient the entire hospital stay (average length of stay [ALOS] 4.2 days). However, multiple MDIs were being dispensed to the same patient. The new program these Black Belts designed allowed one "Common MDI" per floor. MDIs were dispensed to individual patients only when clinically indicated, that is, patients in isolation and/or on mechanical ventilators. Within the first year of the project, pharmacy acquisition costs for MDIs were reduced by $363,000 (a 75% reduction).

Not all BB projects saved this amount of money, but all improved efficiency and reduced waste and many improved quality of care directly.

Examples

The laboratory's Black Belts developed two projects that had a significant effect on turnaround time (TAT) for two tests that are used heavily in the emergency department to determine the severity of a patient's condition. One was for troponin testing that is used to detect myocardial damage and one was for the basic metabolic profile (BMP) testing used for assessing a variety of conditions.

The baseline for troponin testing revealed an average TAT for STAT testing of between 35 and 38 minutes with only 64–68% of the troponins completed in less than 35 minutes, reflecting that as many as 36% of tests were outliers. The team of Black Belts utilized process mapping and collapsed multiple analyzers into one platform and utilized one specimen for multiple assays. The approach reduced the TAT from 36 to 31 minutes and the outliers from 36 to 21% and saved $88,000/year in reagent costs with the change in analyzer use.

The team utilized single-cell process flow and standard work to reduce the TAT on BMP from 35.6 minutes to 22.6 minutes. The time for completion rate for 90% of the tests fell from 54 minutes to 28.9 minutes. This created not only quicker results for the emergency department but also greater capacity for laboratory testing.

One Black Belt example shows the power that the distributed Black Belts had to harness the ideas of the entire workforce, as Toyota says, turning every employee into a scientist.

Example

An environmental services employee in a community health clinic who was on an RIE was excited about the idea of getting rid of waste. He had an idea that the conversion from a regular loop mop to a microfiber mop would save time, money, and improve ergonomics for the employees. He took the idea to one of the community health Black Belts who worked with the employee to pilot the idea. The time mopping an area fell 15%; the employee steps decreased from 1,846 to 246 steps; the ounces of chemicals used fell from 62.5 (cost of $15) to 1.78 ounces (cost of $0.45); the calculated yearly gallons of water used fell from 31,500 to 462 gallons and the pounds lifted per eight-hour shift/employee fell from 1,150 pounds to 20 pounds. The new practice was instituted thanks to one frontline employee and the Black Belt in his area.

Our experience with this cadre of individuals makes us strongly recommend that every organization on a Lean journey create such a group of Lean Black Belts.

ORGANIZATIONAL 5S

The concept and the implementation of 5S are so central to Lean that we must spend some time on its implementation in our organization. Some organizations begin a transformation effort by setting up the proverbial "burning platform." I have always found this a puzzling analogy. I don't know about you, but my instincts would be to get off a burning platform. A logical person could conclude that by the time a platform is burning, you are a little late for meaningful solutions. In contrast to the "burning platform," we wanted to begin our Lean transformation with something fun, something with immediate and obvious benefit to employees and the organization, something that could start the spread of Lean and something that was foundational to Lean. Thus, our Lean journey started with the 160 mid-managers 5S'ing their own areas and reporting the outcome metrics to me in written form (Gabow et al., 2008). The Lean systems improvement department provided the basic supplies for 5S teams. The metrics could be before and after pictures, bags of trash removed, or formal 5S scoring. This created a great opportunity for broad employee engagement. The entire finance department and the entire public health department conducted day-long 5S events (Gabow et al., 2008). The robustness of this simple Lean tool deserves multiple examples, otherwise one might be tempted to dismiss it as simple "house cleaning."

Example

An example of a departmental 5S and its impact on time savings and patient quality is from the respiratory therapy department, which manages the care of patients who require ventilator support and pulmonary therapy such as nebulizer treatments (Gabow et al., 2008). The department operates 24 hours a day/seven days a week and is an equipment-intensive healthcare service utilizing a 1,050-square-foot equipment storage room. The staff was educated about 5S philosophy and process by a Black Belt in the department. The 5S event removed 64 cubic feet of trash (four dumpsters), including old manuals and obsolete supplies; red-tagging of 25 pieces of equipment, including two desks, an equipment washing machine and dryer, and five old ventilators. There were 80 oxygen cylinders from external homecare companies that had migrated into the department, which were now returned. The principles of a visual workplace were utilized to reorganize the equipment. The department used a unique method to assess the impact of a visual workplace by performing a scavenger hunt before and two months after the 5S process. The hunt involved 20 therapists finding 20 randomly selected items from the list of approximately 100 items stored in the respiratory therapy area. The metrics were the number of items found, the time to find them, and the steps taken. The data pre- and post-5S were statistically significantly different. The time to find the 20 pieces of equipment fell from 14.4 minutes before 5S to 8.7 minutes after 5S, a 40% time reduction (p value < 0.0001). Although we would not include this in the financial benefit calculations, this extrapolates to approximately 438 hours per year or 0.21 FTE of lost productivity (and the frustration of hunting and gathering) that now could be focused on patient care. The number of steps needed to find the equipment decreased from 762 to 465 steps per therapist (p value < 0.001). It is important to note that the pieces of equipment which could not be found decreased from 45 before to 1 after 5S. In a real patient care situation, needed equipment would be found, but the searching time would be significant and could clearly delay therapy.

Example

The clinical laboratory department is a large and busy service in any major acute care hospital. It is both an expense and revenue generator and its function has a significant impact on the quality of care. The clinical laboratory's efforts illustrate the power of 5S (Gabow et al., 2008). The administrative director, the head of quality for the laboratory, and another laboratory administrator were Black Belts. The laboratory began its Lean efforts with 5S classes for supervisory and quality committee members, the pathologists, and the management staff. They focused on one area at a time, used daily huddles to reinforce the effort, and praised successes. They instituted a buddy system so no one was in it alone and created a "time to shine" each day. They color-coded all the refrigerated reagents, grouping like reagents, and applied visible expiration dates immediately on opening any reagent. They created visual organization of all the phlebotomy supplies with clear stock rotation. This decreased stock orders by 7% in the face of an 8% increase in procedures. The laboratory team standardized the individual workbenches to create efficient workflow and improved the ergonomics of the work areas (Set in Order).

Overall, they removed 30 dumpsters of old forms and records, 45 dumpsters of small instruments, equipment, and supplies, 35 chairs and stools, and two 6′ × 4′ boxes of hazardous materials and redeployed four file cabinets and two bookcases (saving purchasing new ones).

These efforts magically produced space that the laboratory needed for its expanding testing modalities. The initial effort saved 1,500 square feet and ongoing efforts continued to generate space that enabled a change in location of work areas and large instruments to create efficient workflows. Those moves reduced turnaround time on the STAT centrifuge by 11–19%. The space reclamation permitted space for employee lockers and movement of offices to be in proximity to their areas of supervision.

Considering building laboratory space costs approximately $400/sq ft, this saved $600,000 in construction cost avoidance. The success of this effort gave rise to the space committee implementing the condition that any areas requesting space must provide information on their 5S effort with the formal request for space (Gabow et al., 2008).

A total of 90% of the technical staff and 83% of the pathologists participated in the initial 5S efforts. The ongoing sustainment was led by nonsupervisory staff. This produced employee comments such as:

"Now I come in on weekends and can get straight to work."

"I love not having to travel a football field to get what I need."

Perhaps the laboratory department's greatest reward for their efforts occurred during their accreditation inspection. The inspector who had previously performed an inspection at Denver Health wanted to know when the remodeling project had been completed (there was no remodel, just 5S) and then wanted to learn about 5S.

Although there is not an S for Savings in the 5S algorithm perhaps there should be, as this simple tool not only develops a visual structured workplace; it also saves money.

Example

Engineering was one of the first areas to 5S their storage space. A storage area shown in Figure 7.1 was transformed from disorganized space before 5S to not only an organized space but an effective visual workplace after 5S.

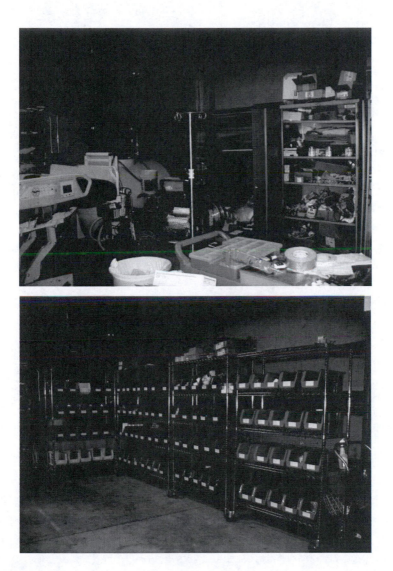

FIGURE 7.1
Engineering storage area before and after 5S.

TABLE 7.2

Engineering Expense Trend

Year	Total Supply Cost	
2004	$1,803,995	Pre 5S
2005	$2,181,408	Pre 5S
2006	$1,652,946	$527,462 improvement from 2005
2007	$1,707,347	$474,061 improvement from 2005
2008	$1,577,110	$604,298 improvement from 2005
2009	$1,567,757	$613,651 improvement from 2005
2010	$1,791,178	$390,230 improvement from 2005
May 2011 Annualized $1,798,414		$382,994 improvement from 2005

This simple tool, as shown in Table 7.2, produced significant savings in engineering. Engineering expense had been increasing as a result of building expansions, new equipment, and inflation as is shown with the $300,000 increase from 2004 to 2005. However, expenses fell from that baseline in 2005 in each year following 5S. This decrease was in the face of a 35% increase in Denver Health's square footage. When inventory areas are poorly organized and something can't be found, another item is frequently ordered. Moreover, poor organization can produce rush orders that escalate the costs even further.

Maybe there should also be an S for Sharing in the 5S steps.

Example

The administrative assistants in the executive suite did a major 5S of the storage area and then advertised on our intranet that any other secretary or clerk could come at certain times and take the extra binders, folders, and the like. The response was huge and the event was fun. We did not calculate the savings, but a new binder costs at least $5.00 and there were at least a hundred of these reclaimed. A small amount of money but dollars add up and it kept what would have been trash out of landfills. Lean is also Green!

The fifth S of Sustain should be audited regularly by someone assigned in the area. It also seems advisable to have regular organizationwide semiannual or annual 5Ss. Moreover, on rounds executives should note whether an area is 5S'ed and any area that lacks an organized visual workplace should be instructed to come up to snuff rapidly. The waste walk in an area at the beginning of an RIE should note the status of the area's 5S.

The impact on every employee is reflected in their comments that ranged from, "Thank you. I now have a place to hang my coat" (little things mean a lot) to "Thank you for showing me this; I 5S'ed my garage." One caveat: one husband 5S'ed his wife's kitchen when she was away, not a good plan. So one 5S rule: don't 5S someone else's space.

EXERCISE

Start your Lean journey with organizationwide 5S. Even if you are already on the journey, do an organizational 5S. This is foundational to Lean and cannot be skipped.

RAPID IMPROVEMENT EVENTS

RIEs are an essential part of a successful Lean journey. Therefore we are providing substantial detail on RIE execution.

Pre-Work

Although the RIE is a one-week intensive and focused problem-solving event, the team cannot come in Monday morning to a completely clean slate. If that happens, you will generate waste, wasted time of six to eight people. The VS steering committee should follow the standard work for RIE preparation, including teeing up RIEs three months in advance and choosing the team at least two months in advance (Appendix Figure A.1). This timing is particularly important for clinicians, nurses, and other healthcare professionals whose work schedules are often set weeks or months in advance. This notice is respectful of the team members and of patients who might have to be rescheduled if short notice were given to a provider.

The VS steering committee should begin filling in the first three boxes of the A3: Reason for Action, Current State, and Target State with baseline and target metrics. If the VS steering committee cannot identify these boxes at a high level, they should ask, "Why are we doing this RIE?" In our parlance, this RIE would likely be a softball. It is important to decide that the process is something that should be done at all. Improving a process of no inherent value is an enormous waste of time, talent, and other resources. For example, you would not want to spend time improving processes such as ordering and performing an MRI for uncomplicated back pain. Other red flags for the success of an RIE are the inability to identify one process owner; inability to identify clear, measureable metrics; or inability to keep the team to six to eight people. These red flags suggest too broad a scope.

In order to define the current state, data need to be gathered in advance. These data often include takt time calculations and cycle time observations. This pre-work does not mean that the RIE team does not fill in these three boxes, but the pre-work provides a starting point that will be confirmed by the team's waste walk, their current state map, and brainstorming on the target state. RIEs have standard work for each team member, for the structure of each of the four days, and for the communication of the work and its outcomes.

Team Members

The RIE team and their duties are:

1. VS Facilitator (in our system a facilitator is from the Lean systems improvement department):
   a. Owns the integrity of the Lean process
   b. Assists, supports, and motivates the process owner, the team lead, and the team members
   c. Conducts pre-work, organizing a preparation meeting in advance
   d. Assists in data gathering such as takt time calculations, and observations of cycle times, work sequences; spends at least eight hours observing the process that is the focus of the RIE
   e. Has drafted boxes 1, 2, 3 of A3
   f. During the RIE week, helps to keep process on track, assists in using Lean tools, makes certain production boards are completed by Tuesday or Wednesday
   g. Conducts post-event work, assisting the process owner with 30-/60-/90-day follow-up
2. Process Owner:
   a. Owns the entire process from preparation, through the RIE, to guaranteeing that the new process is sustained, production boards are in place and utilized, and the metrics collected. This person does not lead the RIE as he may have predetermined ideas

of the problem and its solutions. Occasionally, the process owner may not be a team member, functioning more as a consultant to the RIE team.

b. We learned that there must be only one process owner and that person has to be the individual who is responsible for managing the process/area. One of our most memorable RIE failures was an RIE focusing on patients' lost valuables in the emergency department. Because the valuables could have been lost in the ambulance, in the emergency department, during transport to and from tests, or, for admitted patients, on the hospital unit, everyone was a process owner so no one was responsible and the results were very disappointing.

3. Team Lead:

a. The team lead is responsible for conducting the RIE. She needs to have a good grasp of Lean thinking and tools. The team lead needs to keep the team focused and help guide them to aggressive change. We have found that a Black Belt from another area is an ideal team lead. This individual also attends the 30-/60-/90-day follow-up meetings.

4. Team Members:

a. Team members include individuals who are involved in the process and some individuals who are from other areas. The individuals from other areas often are from areas upstream and downstream of the examined process. Team members can be from external entities such as vendors or individuals from entities linked to the process. For example, we have involved individuals from the fire department in RIEs dealing with the paramedic service or individuals from the state Medicaid agency on RIEs dealing with Medicaid enrollment. Individuals who are from internal upstream or downstream processes and individuals external to the organization are "new eyes" who can ask the 5 whys because they are not committed to the status quo. Individuals from upstream and downstream of the process help everyone understand the flow of the process from what came before to what will come after the process being examined. In keeping with hearing the voice of the customer, it is important to have patients as part of any team that is focusing on a process that interfaces with the patients. They are "new eyes" and certainly can and will ask "why" about many components of the process. Initially, clinical areas can find this uncomfortable and difficult. However, it is an important step to take.

b. Each RIE team should have some old hands and some employees new to the Lean experience. The old hands can keep the process moving and can teach the new individuals. The presence of new participants serves to spread the Lean culture. The team members should span levels of the organizational hierarchy. A C-suite person can be sitting next to a physician and a frontline clerk. Status is checked at the door. Each frontline team member must have received approval from his supervisor to participate. All team members must commit to being present and engaged the entire four days. Often patients can't spend a week, so planning for when it would be most helpful to have them present is important and respectful.

c. We did not provide backfill for the team members while they participated in the RIE except to maintain fixed staffing ratios such as for bedside nurses, paramedics, and others. That meant that among the nonprofessionals others on their work team would be doing more work but these individuals knew they would get their turn to participate in an RIE. For the clinical and administrative professionals this often meant coming in earlier or working later to get their needed tasks done.

d. One group of team members deserves specific comments. Often we are asked questions about if, when, and how to engage physicians in RIE teams. Our answers are:

   i. Physicians must definitely be engaged in the Lean transformation as they drive or are critical participants in many aspects of healthcare that drive quality and cost.

   ii. Physician engagement should begin at the start of the journey. In our model, physician leaders were trained as Black Belts. This training appeals to physicians given its grounding in a scientific method of data acquisition, analysis, and rapid experiments. Physicians also hate wasting their time; explaining this aspect of Lean will get them on board. Training physician leaders not only will get them engaged in Lean thinking and doing but it, in turn, will begin to engage those physicians who report to the leaders.

iii. Physicians should be part of all RIEs that focus on a clinical process. As all other team members, they need to commit to being present for the full RIE week. Clearly, physicians may get called to a patient emergency, but we have encouraged physicians to have coverage as if they were going to be offsite for an academic meeting.

iv. Physician engagement often leads to the question of how to pay them for their time. Denver Health's employed, academic physician model that did not include any bonus plan avoided the need for any additional payment. Therefore, we have no specific guidance on payments. However, there are other nonmonetary rewards that accrued to our physicians and could be an incentive to physicians in other institutions. RIEs specifically, and Lean more broadly, provided an opportunity to use the RIEs as subjects for academic presentations, journal papers, and even as the preliminary data for grant applications. This incentive for academic activity is one that should be emphasized to all healthcare professionals.

5. Consultants:

a. Consultants are internal subject matter experts. During the RIE week questions will arise that no one on the team can answer. This leaves two choices: make a good guess or find the correct answer. Obviously, you need the correct answer. Our expectation was that consultants should be called when needed and they must come. They are needed only briefly and a mutually workable time can be identified. This prevents items either being put on the completion list because of lack of information or from something being decided upon that was not workable. This is a highly efficient and effective solution to the alternative of having everyone at the table for either the entire four days or having a large committee dealing with the issue. An example of the number and range of consultants that are involved in a typical RIE is shown in Table 7.3. As is shown in this table for the asthma RIE, we did occasionally use volunteer external consultants. Clearly, these consultants must be asked in advance and a convenient time for them to interact with the team, either in person or by phone, should be determined.

TABLE 7.3

Example of Consultants Participating in RIE

Clinical Care Process VS/Asthma Care RIE
Director of Community Health Services *(CHS)*
Administrative Director CHS
Pulmonologists from National Jewish Hospital, The Children's Hospital Colorado, and Kaiser Permanente Group
CHS pediatrician, NP, and nurse
HIT application analyst
Patient navigator
Emergency Department/Urgent Care VS/Level 4 Patient Flow
Emergency and urgent physicians, nurses, and emergency department technicians
Security, environmental services, and registration personnel
15 patients, interviewed in rooms

Note: VS—Value Stream.

Structure for RIE Week

The team should meet in a large conference room to facilitate visual display of all the key RIE activities. Ideally, this should be at the location of the process that is being examined. This makes it easy to do the waste walk, to do the rapid experiments, and to communicate and interact with the employees of the area throughout the week. This interaction minimizes surprises for the workforce not on the RIE and hence minimizes pushback.

The RIE is structured to be completed in four days with a report on the morning of day five. The days start at 8:00 a.m. and end at 4:00 p.m. Toyota experimented with the ideal duration of such events and arrived at one week, albeit apparently working night and day (Koenigsaecker, 2013). Although our events were less intense than that, teams ended the week exhausted, but happy. Our COO once said, "The RIE team members go in as strangers and come out as family."

The structure of the week is driven by the problem identification and problem-solving format of the A3. The components of each day are as follows:

Day 1:
> The day starts with a one-hour overview of key aspects of Lean. This is usually done with all the teams for the week at the same time. The details for this training are given above in the Training section of this chapter.

TABLE 7.4

Rules of Behavior for RIE

Be respectful

Check badges at the door; everyone has equal say

Everyone participates

Vegas rules apply

One conversation at a time

Be open to new ideas; there are no bad ideas

Stay focused

Start and stop on time

The teams then go to the site of their specific RIE. They begin with introductions and each member says what they expect to get out of the week. The facilitator discusses the rules of behavior that are listed in Table 7.4.

The teams can, and usually do expand on this basic set of rules. One rule that may strike one as contradictory in relation to the transparency inherent in Lean is the rule, "Vegas Rules Apply." We clearly want RIE dialogue to be respectful, however, it is possible that some comments on process could be interpreted outside the context of the RIE as personal or negative. This rule is to prevent such comments from being passed on, harming the effectiveness of the process.

The RIE enables you to use the Lean tools in a structured manner. Therefore, any Lean tool could be employed during the week. There are some tools that should always be used including 5 whys, waste walk, process map, spaghetti diagrams, and communication circles.

Day 1 is largely about establishing clarity of the current state (also called initial state).

A critical part of standard work for establishing the current state is observing the actual work with a waste walk of the area, documenting the workflow steps and the eight wastes. A current state can never be established without these observations. The current state process map is constructed, identifying non-value-added steps and barriers to flow.

This enables completion of Box 1 and Box 2 and the start of Boxes 3 and 4 of the A3.

Day 2:

Day 2 is largely about defining the target state and the gaps between the current and target states.

In developing the target state the team identifies those non-value-added steps to be eliminated (actually crossing them out on the process map), develops a potential new process, and begins communication of that new process. One way to identify the non-value-added steps is to ask key questions about every step in the mapped process:

"Do I really need this step (or form)?"

"If a customer saw me doing this ... step, would she be willing to pay me to do it?" (Koenigsaecker, 2013).

The team begins designing the new process and starts rapid experiments with the new process, measuring the success (metric verification) and using results to finalize the new process iteratively.

The focus is on Boxes 3, 4, and 5 of the A3.

The executive staff sponsor attends the debrief session at 4:00 p.m.– 5:00 p.m. This is important as Tuesday is usually the hardest day of the RIE week, often dubbed "Terrible Tuesday." At this point, the team thinks they can't possibly complete the task.

Day 3:

Day 3 focuses on completion of rapid experiments, the design of the standard work for the new process, and verification of metrics. The latter two are very important to enable implementation and sustaining of the new process.

The team develops the production board for real time onsite monitoring of the new process.

The focus is on completing Boxes 3, 4, 5, and 6 and beginning box 7 of A3.

Boxes 3, 4, 5, and 6 should tell a seamless story.

Day 4:

The focus is on adjustment and fine-tuning of the new process' standard work.

Create training and training schedule and begin training for work area staff in the new standard work.

The focus is on Boxes 7, 8, and 9 and completion of the A3.

The executive sponsor needs to visit the teams several times during the week in addition to the Tuesday debriefing to make sure the team is staying on track and on task and to help with any barriers that arise during the week.

Day 5:

This is report out and celebration time for all the teams.

TABLE 7.5

Examples of "Just Do Its" from Clinic RIE

Rapid strep cultures stocked in room.
Update "Welcome to the Clinic."
5S provider work area.
Add outgoing fax box.
Add medication refill sheet box.
Eliminate unused supplies in treatment rooms from inventory.
Stock all exam rooms with required forms.
Discontinue printing of recommended vaccines from computer registry.
Reallocate standard work.
Vaccine refrigerator temperature checks from RN to HCP.
Check expiration dates on drugs and supplies from RN to HCP.
Medication refill requests from providers to RN.

The RIE outputs come in several forms. Of course, the main output is the new process. One rule of thumb for the new process that emerges from an RIE is to "halve the bad and double the good" (Koenigsaecker, 2013). This is very effective in creating a substantial target for the week's work.

During the examination of the process there are some things that are obvious, easy, and quick to fix. These are "Just Do Its" and the expectation is that this is what happens. Examples of RIE "Just Do Its" are listed in Table 7.5. One can also think of "Just Do Its" as "Just Stop Its." One might ask, "Who needs an RIE for 'Just Do Its?'" If people are busy doing their day-to-day tasks and have not learned to see waste, the obvious is not seen and not fixed even when it is an easy fix.

Healthcare is in love with forms. That makes forms a particularly likely "Just Stop It." In fact, a good RIE rule is that no team can add a form unless two or three forms are removed. Some observations can lead down paths that are outside the scope of the RIE. It is important both to note these observations in the "parking lot," and to avoid scope creep. The facilitator and the executive staff sponsor should be responsible for making sure creep doesn't occur. One word about parking lots: they can become graveyards. This is a trap we fell into on more than one occasion. The process owner and the facilitator need to make certain these good ideas are not lost and are discussed in the VS steering committee.

Our practice was to cluster three to five RIEs in a week, two weeks of every month. Although this makes these weeks quite busy, it creates a "buzz" and enables the Friday morning report outs to be a celebratory as well as an informational session. The report out of the three to five teams permits team members from across the organization to get a sense of what is happening throughout the organization, creates bonding, breaks down silos, and facilitates the culture change. These report outs provide an opportunity to invite guests who may want to see what Lean looks like on the ground.

Each team reports out the events of the previous four days in a 10-minute standard format using the A3. We found it was helpful to have a visual of all the teams' outputs in the three domains of finance, quality, and human development displayed in the front of the room to emphasize the importance of real deliverables. An example of this is illustrated in Figure 7.2. In this RIE week the four teams were from the emergency department/ urgent care (dubbed first floor), behavioral health, perioperative, and Rocky Mountain Poison and Drug Center VSs. During the presentation of the RIEs from these VSs the information that confirmed the data on this table was presented. Although there was variability in the metrics for the RIEs, they all achieved appropriate outcomes in the three domains. All the RIEs exceeded the financial target of $50,000/RIE and all had employees new to the process participating.

The team lines up for the report and two people usually do the report out: often a first-timer is one of the presenters (human development). Employees are presenting to the leadership of the organization, all the other team members, and often guests. Some employees may have never before spoken in front of a group, it was both scary and empowering. Part

Value Stream	Event	Projected Financial Impact ($)	Quality Metric	Human Development RIE First-Timers
First Floor	ED Patient Admit to Medicine Process	259,063	Cycle Time	6
Perioperative Services	Physician Onboarding and Orientation to the OR	81,355	MDs Affirmed Oriented	4
BHS	Adult Inpatient Discharge Process	105,000	Percent D/C Fees Accurately Coded	5
RMPDC	Invoicing Process Improvement for RMPDC	81,355	Percent First Pass Yield	4
Total	4 RIEs	$526,773	4/4	19

FIGURE 7.2
RIE production report out board.

of the A3 format is detailing the gaps and the wastes in the current process. Standing up in front of the executive team and your colleagues and being proud to detail all the things that were wrong with the process is unusual organizational behavior. This differs radically from two common processes used in healthcare to find out what is wrong: the audit and the mortality and morbidity conference. With these approaches someone else, often a superior or an outside consultant or regulator, points out what is wrong, making the experience quite different from staff identifying problems and creating the solutions themselves. At the end of each 10-minute presentation there is time for praise and questions from the audience. There should always be questions. This is an important part of cultural transformation, being asked hard questions in front of a large group without harshness, but in the spirit of improving and being able to answer without defensiveness also in the spirit of improving.

The insights are in the last A3 slide and these range from funny to profound. The insights listed in Table 7.6 reflect the way in which an RIE generates thoughtful recognition of our shortcomings, shared understanding, problem solving, and the power of the group to create improvement.

The most common insight that we did not add to the list in Table 7.6 is that the process being examined had no standard work. Those of us in healthcare think we have standard processes. This lack of standard process within one institution and across institutions may represent one of the biggest failings of our healthcare system. This undoubtedly contributes to errors, cost, and patient and employee frustration.

Post-Work

Perhaps even more important than pre-work is the post-work inasmuch as post-work involves verifying that the completion plan happened, that the new standard work is being done, that the metrics are displayed in the work area, and that the metrics are being achieved. Improvement only occurs with implementation and sustaining of the new standard. The VS steering committee is tasked with looking back over the last three RIEs in order to guarantee that the post-work is done.

RIE Examples

Denver Health's first RIE was a major success starting the organization out on a positive note.

TABLE 7.6

Examples of Individuals' Insights from RIEs

Wow, we made it!

Inconsistent processes create ambiguity.

Getting the patient's perspective puts the customer in the center of the value equation.

We can overcome obstacles.

RIEs can be flexible and fun.

Lots of opportunities for improvement.

Focus on what we can control.

We don't have to make big changes for big effects.

Ownership brings success.

We all speak a different language.

Assumptions can cost us money.

Our internal consultants taught us a lot.

Including vendors and wholesalers in RIE uncovered many opportunities.

Helps to have outside eyes in the process.

Identifying meaningful metrics never seems to get any easier.

Change is hard, but resistance is futile.

We get caught up in our daily routine without considering more Lean processes.

Obviously conflicting opinions/practices on cancer screening guidelines among family practice, internal medicine, and OB/GYN.

We were not aware that care support was not calling members of every referral.

Everyone gained a better appreciation of the challenges of each other's job.

Didn't realize how frustrated staff was.

Amazed at the amount of work required by one person to get the schedule complete and accurate.

The batching of discharges has significant ramifications to multiple functions throughout the organization.

We enjoy hearing other people's perspectives.

Rapid experiments are beneficial.

Quality of pre-event research significantly affects quality of results.

Problems are now seen as opportunities.

It is amazing what eight people in one room can accomplish in one week.

Example

Postoperative infections represent a significant issue in hospitals. Appropriately timed prophylactic antibiotic administration is an important component in the elimination of such hospital-acquired infections. Denver Health was achieving the appropriate timing of preoperative antibiotics approximately 80% of the time despite numerous efforts to improve this percentage of compliance. An abbreviated version of A3 captures the flow of this first event at a 10,000-foot level and is shown in Figure 7.3 (Hafer, 2012).

1. **Reason for Action**
   SCIP II requires abx within 60 min of "first cut."

2. **Current State**
   Prophylactic abx in OR within 60 min < 80% of cases.

3. **Target State**
   Prophylactic abx in OR within 60 min in 100% of cases.

4. **Gap Analysis**
   Abx given "OCTOR" Variable abx APC Frustration OR Frustration.

5. **Solution Approach**
   Conduct waste walk. Map process RIE to include IC Chart review.

6. **Rapid Experiment**
   Change OCTOR to "Abx delivered in OR by anesthesiologist." Abx guidelines.

7. **Completion Plans**
   Change order forms. Monitor data.

8. **Confirmed State**
   "We've changed our practice."

9. **Insights**
   The problem was definitely the process, not the people!

FIGURE 7.3
A3 perioperative antibiotic administration.

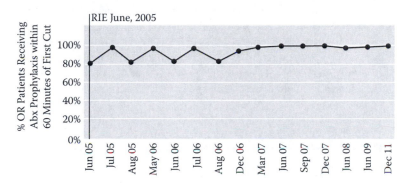

FIGURE 7.4
Surgical site infection RIE results.

Because this is an abbreviated version all the data elements that would be in boxes and the details of the rapid experiments are not included.

Actually mapping the process with a team doing the work created an "Aha moment:" the anesthesiologist was the only one who really knew when it was within an hour of cut-time. Therefore, within a week the antibiotic administration was changed from "On call to the OR (OCTOR)," to the anesthesiologist administering the antibiotics (abx in Figure 7.3) in the OR. The results are illustrated in Figure 7.4 and underscore the critical aspect of the active monitoring of outcomes. Dips in outcomes continued to occur as might be expected in one's first foray into Lean. At this point we did not understand all the Lean tools that prevent this type of backsliding. However, Lean provides a disciplined way to establish the root cause (such as old forms slipping in), take counteractions, and strengthen standard work and visual management. Once we learned to apply all of these approaches effectively, the goal of antibiotics within one hour of cut-time was achieved 100% of the time and was maintained for years, undoubtedly preventing postoperative infections and even saving patients' lives.

The overwhelming majority of RIEs were in VSs, however, we had an occasional free-standing RIE that was not part of a current VS. These events focused on some flawed process whose improvement would facilitate patient flow. When such an RIE was approved by the Lean systems improvement department, an executive sponsor, facilitator, and process owner were assigned and metrics developed and tracked.

Example

Patient transportation is happening every hour of every day in an acute care setting. However, we had not defined the hospital's transportation needs or set the priorities for the resources. The current state revealed multiple delays, improper modes of transportation, and underutilization of other available resources. The rapid experiments resulted in standard work for patient preparation, new processes for transporting laboratory specimens that utilized other current resources, and the establishment of staggered request times for patient transport to and from dialysis. These interventions increased the transports/hour/transporter from 2.2 to 2.6, increased the trips/transporter/year from 4,576 to 5,400. This reduced the need for additional transporters to meet demand and increased patient and caregiver satisfaction.

APPLYING DESIGN TOOLS

There is an array of other tools in the Lean tool box that seasoned Lean enterprises can use. It is not our intention to cover the entire array. However, there are three more advanced tools that we have found helpful even at the early stage of our Lean journey. These are the design or planning tools. They include 3P, 2P, and Vertical VSs.

With our sensei guidance we conducted approximately 50 3P and 2P events in the design of new buildings and new space, respectively. Utilizing 3P or 2P tied together the least waste way of space design with a new least waste way of working. This is in contrast to one of the more common approaches to construction that involves all the stakeholders advocating for what they want, usually expanding the space to conform to the current dysfunctional, or at least an unexamined process.

2P can be utilized for space that is already constructed but is being assigned a new use or for altering the layout of existing space to fit a "Leaned" VS (Koenigsaecker, 2013). This was used successfully in the redesign of the pediatric intensive care unit, the move of pediatric operative procedures from the main operating room to the operating rooms in the obstetrics area, and for a temporary move of the surgical intensive care unit during major reconstruction of the existing unit. The pediatric surgeon who had practiced in multiple academic institutions stated the use of this process for the move of pediatric surgery was the smoothest transition he had ever experienced.

Our use of the vertical VS approach which is described in Chapter 5 was more limited than was our use of 3P and 2Ps. We used this approach for improving our cancer screening, the creation of a centralized patient contact center, the beginning of a new HIT implementation, and the implementation of a large grant from the Center for Medicare and Medicaid Innovation.

COMMUNICATION

Communication is important in any initiative, but is critical with the introduction of a new way of thinking about doing work. The majority of the communications pathways are the same as they would be for any initiative. However, there may be some unique aspects. The Lean journey did have some different audiences than might occur with some other institutional healthcare initiatives. Because of the newness of Lean in healthcare and its emphasis on waste and quality, we wanted to disseminate information about our Lean journey to city and state governments, payers, foundations, and the business community. Others should consider these as their audiences as well in communicating their Lean journey.

Clearly, one of the key audiences was our board. The most effective communication to the board was done by the RIE teams. Every other month one of the teams presented their A3 report out to the board. The enthusiasm, pride, and outcomes that were conveyed by frontline staff convinced the board of the power of Lean more than did any graphs or charts. You can imagine the impact on a group of frontline staff who were given the opportunity to speak before the board and being congratulated for detailing the problems they found and fixed.

The communication to the entire staff began with the employee focus groups described in Chapter 2. In the beginning years a specific publication with focus on Lean was produced regularly. Frequent CEO columns on Lean appeared in our monthly employee newsletter and Lean was highlighted in the annual CEO's address on the State of Denver Health. This address occurred during our annual Day of Celebration. One other aspect of that day was a poster session with a special component for Lean entries, which produced 25–35 posters per year. All posters were displayed during the day and awards were given for the best posters.

Production boards throughout the organization and having huddles at the production boards highlighted Lean accomplishments and the role of everyone in maintaining the improvement. Executives focusing on the production boards on their rounds had a similar communication function.

As in all organizations, the employees themselves are a robust source of communication, often faster than any formal communication. The 250 Black Belts, the 2,000 employees who had been on RIEs, and the teams at the Friday report provided employees with firsthand experience that facilitated the creation of a culture of Lean.

8

Metrics, Reporting, and Information Archiving

METRICS

As with most "old saws," the "old saw" that you can only manage what you measure is true. Thus, metrics are an important part of the Lean journey. Although one should not equate measurement with improvement, you cannot improve without the measurement of what is important. Vince Lombardi is quoted as saying, "If you aren't keeping score, you are just practicing." We didn't want our Lean journey to be just practice; we wanted it to be the real thing. This makes metrics important. Metrics, more accurately the right metrics, are essential for a number of reasons:

- To allow the alignment of all organizational activities around what is important
- To document what works and what doesn't; only then can you improve by spreading what works and discarding or fixing what hasn't worked
- To permit calculation of ROI
- To educate managers about financial management and the business case for quality
- To facilitate transparency
- To enable celebrating success

As discussed in the Tools to Create Prioritization and Alignment section in Chapter 5, metrics cascade from the system level to frontline processes through VS and RIE metrics. Organizational goals determine the system metrics; the system metrics inform the choice of VSs; VS metrics dictate the metrics for individual RIEs. This cascading of metrics creates organizational alignment and cascades the goals from the leadership level to the frontline staff that are in the RIEs. At all three levels there should be at least three types of metrics: financial, quality, and human development. The system metrics are established yearly by the executive team and the VS steering team committee established their metrics yearly as part of the VS analysis/mapping and submitted those metrics to the CEO for approval. One challenging question in establishing any metric is "How high to aim?" Those very experienced in Lean would say that full utilization of Lean can produce a fourfold yield in productivity and a reduction of errors by 99% (Koenigsaecker, 2013). That takes time to achieve and it won't happen in year one or even year two. Even with that caveat, I don't know anyone in healthcare who would aim that high. One role of the CEO is to push for higher rather than lower goals. Moreover, given Toyota's consistently high performance, there is no reason to think that one year's high level of performance at either the system or VS level should not be just as high or higher the next year.

Establishing metrics that reflect the intervention and are easily and accurately obtained is not as simple as it may appear. One might think that the generally high level of training within healthcare would make understanding metrics easier than in factory settings. However, establishing metrics at the VS and RIE level is a challenge (the system level seems to be easier). This is, in part, due to the complexity of healthcare, which often leads to the question of "What is within a VS's span of control?" For example, the revenue cycle VS could not have a metric of the simplification of the state's Medicaid enrollment process nor could the behavioral health VS have a goal of increasing state mental health beds (no matter how much they might wish for that). There is a tendency initially to see solutions, and thus metrics, outside one's own backyard. The metric must reflect the process that the group is trying to change. Measuring the metrics should not require a great deal of time and effort, generating new waste. Despite the growing robustness of electronic data in healthcare, there is still much desired information that is not readily available or, if available, requires analysis to get a true picture.

Financial Metrics

Financial metrics present their own challenges that are listed in Table 8.1.

Some may say that financial metrics should not be included or emphasized, believing that it makes quality less important. However, given the

TABLE 8.1

Challenges in Establishing Financial Metrics

What are you going to count as money?
• Hard green dollars
• Cost avoidance
• New revenue
Who decides what is counted as money?
Can department use its own savings?
Do the savings lower next year's budget?
If unneeded positions are identified, will those individuals be laid off?

issues that cost presents to American healthcare and the consequences that cost generates, this seems off the mark. Moreover, eliminating waste should produce both positive financial and quality outcomes: they should be linked. Finally, for a safety net institution, like Denver Health, financial viability is a keystone of access and, hence, quality for thousands of vulnerable individuals.

In establishing financial metrics, a first step is to decide what you are counting as money. Are you counting only savings or are you using a broader definition? Denver Health used a broader definition. Financial benefit was Denver Health's financial metric and it included savings (dollars that did not go out the door) and two measures of revenue increases: increased productivity with the same resources or increased revenue accrued from a new or Lean-improved process. An example of the latter was the increased revenue from the increased number of uninsured patients who were enrolled in Medicaid. Although this did not save the government money directly, it did enable Denver Health to continue to expand the number of uninsured patients it cared for while remaining solvent.

You also need to decide at the beginning if you will accept only hard dollars. Our CFO's standard was "Hard, green dollars that crossed her palm." We did not count "soft money." For example, a new process that saved 15 minutes of a clerk's or nurse's time would not be counted unless the change saved that amount of time for enough employees to permit a decrease in the number of employees needed. Cost avoidance was not generally counted. However, there were exceptions. For example, the Denver Health's paramedic ambulance fleet had established a standard for vehicle replacement that had been utilized for many years. The Lean efforts enabled lengthening the time frame, saving actual cash and, therefore, this was counted as a savings.

It is important to establish who actually decides what is saved. At Denver Health the financial benefit determinations went through several layers of scrutiny. The RIE teams' and Black Belts' financial benefit calculations were first reviewed by a financial analyst assigned to Lean and then by the associate CFO. The final endorsement of these calculations came from the CEO, occasionally in consultation with the CFO, if there were dilemmas.

Every department, particularly in a safety net institution, has needs they would like to address and initiatives they would like to undertake. This gives rise to the question, "If my department saves money, can we use it for what we need (meaning for what hasn't been approved in the budget)?" With rare exceptions, our answer to that was, "No." This answer may not be possible at all institutions, but Denver Health employees are unusually focused on the organizational mission and individual employees and departments took pride in what they contributed to the whole. Other questions related to the calculation of the financial benefits are, "What is the impact on next year's budget from this year's Lean savings?" and "Do the savings lower the next year's budget?" Our simple answer was, "Yes, it does lower next year's budget, unless new initiatives or new costs are approved in the budget process." The zeal for seeing waste and the underlying culture of our institution mitigated this as a problem.

A similar question that reflects both human development and financial management is, "If a process is improved and less people are needed, will we need to lay them off?" The answer to that was a solid, "No." It seemed quite clear that there would be few eager participants in Lean if the outcome of individuals' efforts were a loss of their jobs. Therefore, at the beginning of our Lean journey, the board stated that there would be no layoffs related to Lean improvements. However, they were equally clear that layoffs, although always a last resort, could occur if the financial situation of the institution changed.

There was no bonus system for anyone including the executives and no physician practice plan or physician bonuses at Denver Health. A team award program, based on savings or quality improvements, had been established independent of Lean. Team awards were given to groups of individuals who had come together to solve a problem. For a team to receive an award, they needed to demonstrate either significant financial savings or quality improvements from their team efforts with clear metrics. These awards were small amounts of money, but they clearly resulted from outcomes within the employees' span of control as opposed to many bonus systems that distribute some amount of money to employees based on organizational financial outcomes. Teams were encouraged to submit Lean efforts, including RIEs or Black Belt efforts for these team awards. More than 600 employees received awards for their Lean efforts.

Not only are the right metrics important, but targets related to those metrics are also important. "Humans simply cannot display creativity or the will to meet challenges when they cannot see the goal" (Hino, 2002). Each VS and each Black Belt had yearly targets. The financial targets and actual financial impact for 2012 of the Black Belts and the VSs are displayed in Table 8.2. The Black Belts and 13 of the formal VSs and areas functioning as VSs exceeded their targets. Three did not. RMPDC VS shortfall was due to the timing of the addition of the second VS in the area that had a yearly target of $620,000. The OB shortfall related to a marked decrease in the number of deliveries, which reflected the national trend that occurred with the recession and was magnified at Denver Health due to deliveries to immigrants. It also reflected a method change for the calculation. The human resources department had approval for a new initiative that reduced their savings. Specialty clinics started very late in the year and therefore had no target and had little realization of financial benefit.

TABLE 8.2

2012 VS and Black Belt Targets and Impacts

VS	2012 Targets	2012 Impacts
Black Belts	$7,110,000	$7,418,511
Revenue Cycle	$6,000,000	$9,664,739
CHS (2)	$1,300,000	$1,794,648
OB	$1,000,000	$216,569
BHS	$470,000	$726,284
ED/Adult Urgent Care	$1,100,000	$1,890,626
Clinical Process	$200,000	$326,736
HR	$520,000	$175,090
RMPDC (2)	$3,620,000	$3,054,772
Managed Care	$2,630,000	$6,305,285
Pharmacy	$1,200,000	$4,479,482
Periop	$2,000,000	$2,921,682
Nursing	$1,000,000	$1,536,414
eHS	$2,500,000	$4,643,717
Paramedics	$3,000,000	$4,147,945
Supply Chain	$1,500,000	$1,886,053
Specialty Clinic	—	$11,414
Total	$35,770,000	$51,199,968

However, the overall financial benefit is quite impressive. It is remarkable that despite a target of $35.7 million, the actual impact exceeded that by more than $15 million. This is even more remarkable when you realize that the Black Belts and the VSs had already produced more than $120 million in institutional financial benefit in the preceding three years.

Quality Metrics

The quality metrics in a healthcare institution are likely to generate fewer questions or issues than the financial metrics. However, as the national quality initiatives have demonstrated, it can be challenging to establish meaningful and easily measurable metrics. National data, particularly the University Healthsystem Consortium data, were used for a range of institutional and departmental quality metrics at Denver Health. These metrics included global institutional outcomes such as observed to expected mortality and observed to expected mortality for individual departments such as surgery, medicine, and obstetrics. The metrics also focused on nationally targeted events such as ventilator-associated pneumonia, central-line infections, postoperative deep venous thrombosis, and readmission rate. Important preventive measures such as immunization and cancer screening were also followed. Many, but not all, of the metrics were benchmarked to national data and were not linked to a particular VS or RIE. However, it was important to document that not only did these broad quality measures not worsen, but also that they improved with our Lean efforts. Many of these quality outcomes are delineated in Chapter 9. Some specific quality metrics for various VSs and component RIEs are shown in Tables 8.3A and B. For example, in community health services, the overall quality metric was improved performance on its detailed ambulatory quality scorecard, which contained an array of metrics related to the specific disciplines within CHS. One RIE within CHS focused on asthma care and an ambulatory quality scorecard metric for that was the percentage of children with persistent asthma who were on controller medication. This underscores the attempt to have RIE metrics roll up to VS metrics.

Human Development Metrics

Metrics of human development are important for the Lean journey. For Toyota, developing employees was foundational as reflected in

TABLE 8.3A

Examples of Value Stream Quality Metrics

Value Stream Quality Metrics	
Value Stream	**Quality Metric**
Revenue Cycle	Aggregate Clean Registration Score, Clean Claims Rate
Paramedics	Percentage of Intubated Patients with PetCo2 Monitor
Behavioral Health Services	Treatment Plan Updates
Clinical Process	AHRQ PE/DVT Rate
Community Health Services	Ambulatory Quality Scorecard
Human Resources	Employee Turnover Rate
OB/GYN	Trimester of Entry into Prenatal Care, Mortality Rate
RMPDC	First Pass Yield
Perioperative Services	PACU Pt Discharge Instructions Complete
Pharmacy	Inpatient Clinical Interventions
Managed Care	ED Visits per 1,000 Encounters
Supply Chain	Central Supply Stock Outs (as percent of units issued)

their often-quoted saying: "We build people before we build cars" (Koenigsaecker, 2013).

Two goals were at the center of our human development metrics: empowering all employees with knowledge, information, and the opportunity to contribute; and embedding Lean in the culture. A simple measure reflecting these goals was the number of employees in a given RIE who were new to the process. This may seem simplistic (and it is), but others have endorsed this as a key human development metric based on Toyota seeing these week-long events as a prime learning opportunity (Koenigsaecker, 2013). In 2012, 216 employees participated in an RIE for the first time. Metrics reflecting the embedding of Lean into the culture are found in the results of the employee survey displayed in Table 8.4. Of the surveyed employees 83% stated they understood Lean philosophy and how it helped maintain our mission by reducing waste. Employees who had participated in at least one RIE were statistically more likely to be positive on a wide range of questions on morale, commitment, and satisfaction underscoring what an empowering tool an RIE is. A qualitative measure of human development can be found in the insights provided in the RIE report outs (see Table 7.6). Another measure of employee development is the year-over-year increase in financial benefit per Black Belt as it reflects not only their increasing sophistication in seeing waste but also their engagement in the process.

TABLE 8.3B

Rapid Improvement Event Quality Metrics

Value Stream	Rapid Improvement Event Topic	Quality Metric
Community Health Services	Asthma Care	Percentage of Persistent Asthmatics on Controller Medications
Clinical Process	Inpatient Diabetes Care–Order Sets	Number of Glucose-Related Safety Events per Month (<50 or >400 mg/dL)
Managed Care	Long-Term Care	Reduced Readmissions
Revenue Cycle	Incorrect Date of Service	Accounts Needing Correction
Pharmacy	Charge Master Description Process	Defects and Errors in PDM/CDM
		Duplicate Drugs, Deleted in PDM, Still in CDM
		PDM Drug Name Not Found in CDM
Managed Care	90-Day Maintenance Drugs	Getting Needed Prescription Drugs
Managed Care	"Take Control" of Disease Management	Percentage Increase in Eligible Members with AIC <9
		Percentage Increase in Eligible Members with BP <140/90
Clinical Process	Outpatient Chronic Pain Standardized Management	Use of Pretreatment Risk Assessment Tools
Rocky Mountain Poison and Drug Center	External Specialty Referral Process	First Pass Yield of Referral Forms-Completed and No Additional Info Needed

TABLE 8.4

Results of 2012 Employee Survey Regarding Lean

85% Employee Response Rate
- I have participated in an RIE   **44%**
- I see the benefits of Lean Process in driving the right process at DH   **69%**
- I understand the Lean philosophy and how it reduces waste in our institution   **83%**

Although establishing metrics and targets are critical for success, success will only be achieved if outcomes are measured, examined, create accountability, are transparent, and ultimately change processes and behaviors. The financial and quality metrics were maintained in a large database that listed each VS and every financial and quality metric for each RIE. The metrics were updated monthly and reviewed in a meeting with the CEO, the director of the Lean systems improvement department, the Lean financial analyst, and the associate CFO. Metrics that failed to meet target were followed up with the process owner or executive staff by one of these team members, often in the form of a question from the CEO. If targets had been achieved and were maintained for six months, reporting was moved to quarterly and then to every six months. If maintained for more than a year, the measurement was often dropped. In some instances, if the target was not at a national benchmark, such as days in accounts receivable, the target was raised to be closer to the benchmark.

REPORTING

Measurement enables you to know where you have been and where you need to go. It is most helpful and we would say, only helpful, when the information is shared. The target metrics for the enterprise and for each VS were posted on individual boards in the main conference room of the institution that was used for all large internal meetings and many meetings with external groups. A red, yellow, or green circle was placed on the individual value stream boards if the VS outcomes for these metrics were less than 80% of target, greater than 80% but less than target, or at or above target, respectively. Transparency at the enterprise level is important in conveying organizational commitment. It also reinforces that the journey to perfection is ongoing. Although this level of organizational transparency is necessary, it is not sufficient for daily improvement and problem solving. Visual management (discussed in detail in Chapter 5) with real-time metrics in the areas where work is done is critical. A component of this is to have each area's VS map posted in that work area. This gives all employees an understanding (often for the first time) of the entire workflow of their processes. We believe that the transparency of data should be broadly inclusive. For example, in the main hallway of the

Medical ICU, the real-time data on ventilator-associated pneumonia was posted not only for employees, but also for families to see.

Real-time visual metrics are only helpful if they are used. Standard work for using them must be created and followed. For example, the board with the area's metrics can and should be used at the location of the beginning of shift huddle. This was used effectively in the community health clinics, the operating room, the pediatric service, and the obstetrics services.

Individual departments reported their Black Belts and VS efforts (if they were part of a VS) in specific Lean sections of their annual reports.

INFORMATION ARCHIVING

One of the factors in Toyota's success was the documentation within the company of their efforts (Hino, 2002). We believe this type of documentation enabled the spread of ideas and created an archive of our learning. To accomplish this, the information needed to be readily accessible. The stored documentation related to three areas: rapid improvement and other events, Black Belt initiatives, and metrics for Lean activities. We chose to organize the information primarily by VS and stored the information on our internal information system. Every VS had an individual folder. All the Lean activities (VSA, RIEs, 2 and 3Ps) within the VS were organized chronologically and included all the A3s and associated information. The database was maintained by the Lean systems improvement department on a SharePoint site.

A portal was developed with a standard template for all Black Belt reports (Appendix Figure A.2). The database could be sorted by Black Belt name or date of submission and was accessible to every Black Belt.

Financial metrics for Black Belt initiatives, RIEs, and VSs were tracked and posted by the finance department in a file and these files were sent to the person responsible for these efforts.

9

Outcomes and Lessons Learned

OUTCOMES

The financial results of the Black Belt efforts, expressed as average savings per Black Belt, over a three-year time frame and the cumulative financial benefit for all the Black Belts over the period of our Lean effort are displayed in Figures 9.1 and 9.2, respectively.

The $30,000 target for each Black Belt was established in the fourth full year of our Lean journey in 2009. As shown in Figure 9.1, in that year the average financial benefit per Black Belt exceeded the target, reaching $50,000. Two years later the average financial benefit per Black Belt had reached $110,000, over three times the target. The 20 highest dollar values achieved in a year by any individual Black Belt ranged from $130,000 to $770,000. These 20 individuals were distributed throughout the organization including correctional care, managed care, pharmacy, nursing, public relations, and a variety of other Denver Health components. Many of these individuals had been in their positions for years. They were smart and committed to the organization, our mission, and our patients. Yet, they had not delivered savings of this magnitude in previous years. The Black Belt total financial benefit reached $42.5 million by 2012, reflecting the increase in number of Black Belts over time and the average increase in financial benefit per Black Belt. In addition to this impressive financial benefit, they created thousands of process improvements that were reflected in the more than 1,500 Black Belt reports that were submitted. These improvements affected quality, the patient experience, and the employees' work lives. This is a persuasive example of the incredible power of training our leaders in the philosophy and tools of Lean. This also demonstrates that those trained to see waste can find plenty of it anywhere within our organizations. Of note, there was almost no expense for these

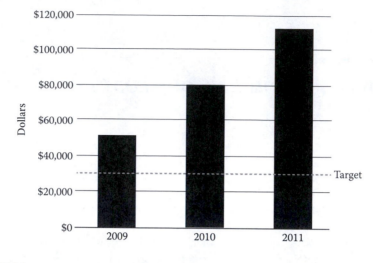

FIGURE 9.1
Average financial benefit per Black Belt.

250 individuals using Lean every day to reduce waste. After the first year, the training was primarily done by the Lean department and there was no backfill for the trainees' time.

Given that VSs and their RIEs examine broader processes than is the norm for Black Belt efforts, the total financial benefit is greater from these activities. The cumulative financial benefits for the VSs exceeded $152 million.

By the first full year of our Lean journey one VS exceeded $1 million of financial benefit. By the fourth full year of our journey six VSs exceeded $1 million and one had exceeded $10 million of financial benefit. By the seventh full year 15 VSs exceeded $1 million in financial benefit. Clearly, not all VSs achieved the same financial outcomes. This likely reflected a number of factors including the timespan over which a particular VS existed (e.g., revenue cycle was a VS throughout our entire Lean journey) and the number of RIEs that VS had per year.

The total cumulative financial benefit for Black Belts and VSs over the years of our Lean effort is displayed in Figure 9.3. There are a number of observations that can be made from Figure 9.3. The first is that the financial benefits increased slowly at the start of the Lean journey. By year 3, the increase per year became greater, reaching over $50 million in the sixth full year. This likely reflects a number of factors including increased numbers of VSs and Black Belts, increasing skill with applying Lean, more sen-

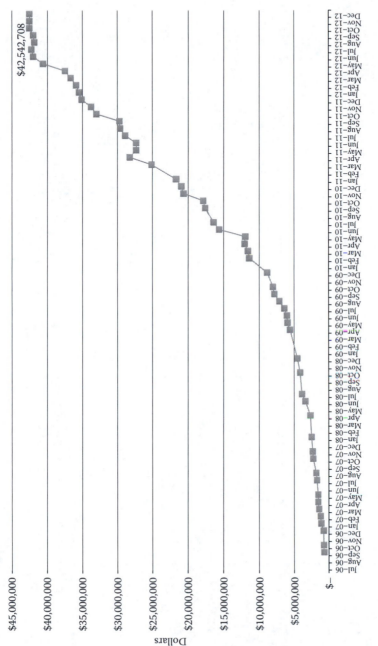

FIGURE 9.2

Cumulative Black Belt financial benefit.

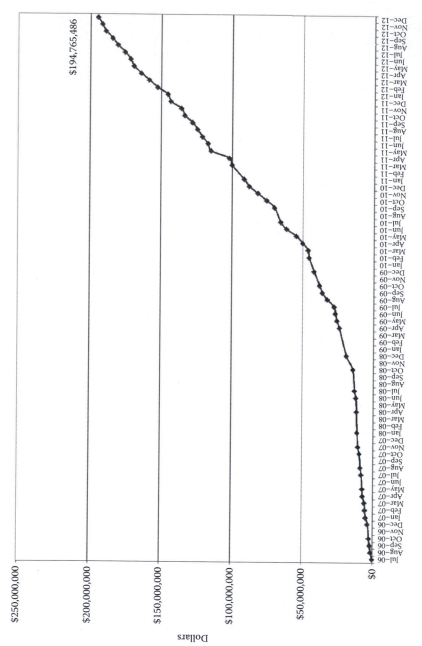

FIGURE 9.3

Cumulative Black Belt and RIE financial benefit.

sei engagement, and having had a sufficient number of RIEs in each VS to improve processes significantly and reduce waste.

The financial benefit in the latter years demonstrates that there is a large reservoir of waste to tap. The idea that the financial benefits would level off after getting the low-hanging fruit is not applicable to the Lean approach to seeing and removing all waste. The continued financial benefit over time is illustrated by Toyota's and other manufacturing companies' results over many years.

The examples of quality of care ranged from overall mortality data (Figure 9.4) to areas of national focus such as central-line infections (Figure 9.5) and surgical site infections (Figure 9.6) to primary and secondary

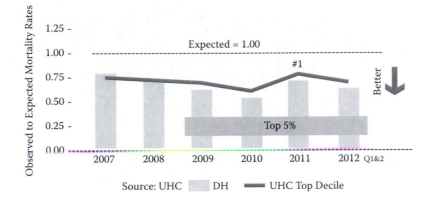

FIGURE 9.4
Overall inpatient mortality index. (From UHC Clinical Data Base/Resource Manager™. Used by permission UHC. All rights reserved.)

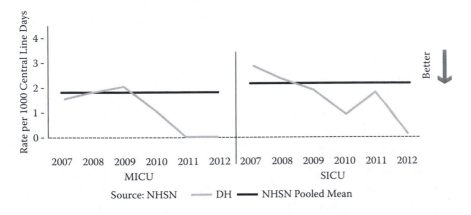

FIGURE 9.5
Central-line associated bloodstream infections.

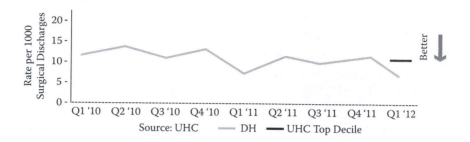

FIGURE 9.6

Overall surgical site infection rate. (From UHC Clinical Data Base/Resource Manager™. Used by permission UHC. All rights reserved.)

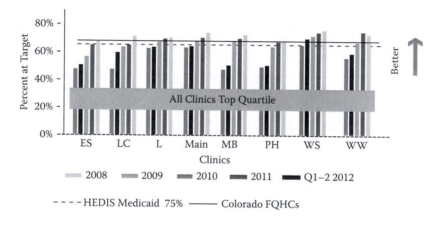

FIGURE 9.7

Hypertensive blood pressure control.

prevention (Figures 9.7 through 9.9). It is not possible to prove that all of these clinically important quality improvements emanated directly from the Lean efforts. However, increased access to primary care and behavioral health services (data not shown), increased preventive screening for cancer (Figure 9.8), increased immunization (Figure 9.9) and use of dental varnish application in children (data not shown), decreased deep venous thrombosis occurrences (Figure 4.1) and timely administration of preoperative antibiotics (Figure 7.4), and decreased readmissions (Figure 9.10) were specific foci of Lean activities. This suggests a causal link between the application of Lean in clinical processes and the increased quality of those processes. The quality of care outcomes are particularly impressive given the highly vulnerable populations cared for by Denver Health.

In reflecting on the quality outcomes, one could hypothesize that removing wasteful process steps that use resources, adding standard

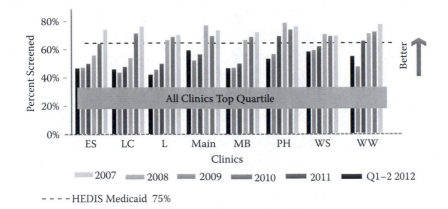

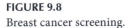

FIGURE 9.8
Breast cancer screening.

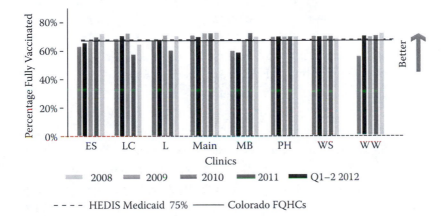

FIGURE 9.9
Pediatric immunization (Combo 3).

work, creating mistake proofing, jidoka, and andon pulls, and managing with visual cues would lead to improved quality and better patient outcomes throughout the clinical enterprise. Most importantly, the overall quality data demonstrate that realizing almost $200 million of financial benefit was not accompanied by decreased quality but actually an improvement in standard, benchmarked quality metrics. This is a critically important observation because such an outcome is not a likely hypothesis for more usual cost-cutting measures.

The number of employees trained as Black Belts and the number of employees who participated in RIEs are important human development

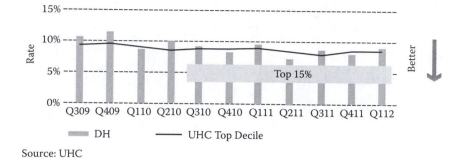

Source: UHC

FIGURE 9.10

30-day all cause readmission rate. (From UHC Clinical Data Base/Resource Manager™. Used by permission UHC. All rights reserved.)

measures. Perhaps the best overall measure of employee engagement is the employee survey results that were shown in Table 8.4. The one limitation of this measure is that it was performed only once every other year.

One human resource metric, albeit not necessarily a human development metric, used by some institutions that have pioneered Lean in healthcare is the redeployment of individuals after a process has had the waste removed and fewer individuals are needed (Koenigsaecker, 2013). Some experienced Lean practitioners believe that in a circumstance in which the new process requires fewer people that the people should be immediately redeployed to the Lean department until another position is identified. The basis for this recommendation is that if you keep the people, the process will quickly slip back to the way it was done previously, utilizing those individuals. In organizations that espouse this approach, they emphasize that it is the best people from the area who should be redeployed. This can be an option offered for volunteers from the area. We did not adopt this immediate redeployment approach. Although there were RIEs that produced a new process that required either fewer people or a different mix of people, we rarely redeployed individuals as there were often vacant positions that then were not filled and there was sufficient turnover in most areas to accommodate these changes.

The financial, quality, and human development results of Denver Health's Lean journey present a strong case for the power of Lean, particularly in a safety net institution that faces many challenges in resources and a vulnerable population that may not be present in many other healthcare institutions. It is important to note that other pioneers in Lean in healthcare have demonstrated equally impressive outcomes. Many of Virginia Mason's successes are documented in *Transforming Healthcare: Virginia Mason Medical Center's Pursuit of the Perfect Patient Experience* (Kenny, 2011) and more recently in *Accelerating Health Care Transformation with Lean and Innovation: The Virginia Mason Experience* (Plsek, 2014). Similarly, some of ThedaCare's successes are detailed in *On the Mend: Revolutionizing Healthcare to Save Lives and Transform the Industry* (Toussaint and Gerard, with Adams, 2010). Other institutional successes are documented in a variety of other sources (Joint Commission Resources, 2008; Hafer, 2012). The many examples provided by a range of healthcare entities underscore the utility and replicability of Lean throughout healthcare. Lean's use is not limited to manufacturing and healthcare. Lean is an effective philosophy and tool for government entities as well (Miller, 2013). As a result of exposure to our Lean efforts, Denver Water, Denver International Airport, the City and County of Denver, and the state of Colorado are currently engaged in Lean.

LESSONS LEARNED

In keeping with the Lean precept of continuous improvement and Toyota's belief in reflection, we learned many lessons on our Lean Journey. These are listed in Table 9.1.

There a number of components of our Lean journey that seem to have contributed to Denver Health's success in using Lean. Of course, there are also reflections on what would have improved our journey. Elaboration on both of these may be useful.

Having a True North destination that was noble, important, and a stretch, inspired our employees to engage in the journey.

Belief in the philosophy and principles of Lean is essential. The Lean tools are wonderful and, even used in isolation, will bring about some improvements. However, Lean can only achieve its true power if it is viewed in the context of its core philosophy and principles. The pillars of respect for people—all people, the workers, the patients, the population—and continuous improvement enable system transformation.

TABLE 9.1

Lessons Learned

Contributors to Success

A noble, important, and a stretch True North
Belief in philosophy and principles of Lean
Sensei guidance
Engagement and commitment of leadership
Disciplined implementation structure
Application of key Lean tools
Cadre of Black Belts
Cadre of Lean facilitators
Rapid improvement events are "remarkable social invention"
Aggressive pace and widespread employee involvement
Patience
A3 is powerful
Measurement, accountability, and transparency
Teaching others helped us learn
Applying for awards helped us assess our journey

What Could Have Improved Our Lean Journey

Having a full-time sensei from the beginning
More in-depth training for our leadership
Greater hands-on learning for our leadership
Following our own Lean standard work always
Early, greater, and more effective use of takt time, visual management, and model flow cells
Sharing our journey more often and more formally

Sensei guidance provides the deep knowledge and experience needed to do Lean effectively. As in any discipline, having someone with mastery enables the student to achieve goals that would not otherwise be possible. Engagement and commitment of leadership is a must. One of the gurus of Lean implementation has said, "I think of Lean as exceptionally powerful, but also as exceptionally *leadership-intensive*" [our emphasis] (Koenigsaecker, 2013). We emphatically agree with this assessment.

In healthcare this leadership intensity must begin with the CEO and include the executive team, the key administrative directors, the nursing leadership, and the physician leadership. Our employed academic physicians provided a powerful resource for our Lean journey. The engagement and commitment of the leadership must be grounded in belief in the philosophy and principles of Lean and must be translated into meaningful participation in the whole array of implementation. Although a

Lean systems improvement department offers structural support, assigning Lean solely to a person or a department will not succeed any more than achieving institutional quality can occur solely from having a quality department.

I once was asked by a senior manager, after a lecture, what she should do if she wanted to do Lean but the CEO was not interested. My response was, "Either forget about implementing Lean or find a new job at an institution where the CEO was committed to Lean." Others have had similar responses to this type of question (Liker, 2004).

The critical role of leadership underscores the vulnerability of transformation to leadership transitions and is reflected in Toyota's long-standing policy of promotion of individuals deeply steeped in the Lean culture (Liker, 2004). This strategy has sustained their philosophy and approach over decades. In the healthcare sector, ThedaCare has developed a defined approach for succession planning to guarantee unbroken continuation of their Lean journey when CEOs transition (Toussaint and Gruner, 2013).

A disciplined implementation structure focused on VSs enables delivering value on demand without waste. Randomly using Lean tools and conducting random RIEs that are not connected to the flow of a VS can yield some results. These have been termed "random acts of Lean" (Chalice, 2007). However, just as random acts of kindness produce some good, such random acts cannot achieve what a focused disciplined commitment to kindness can achieve. Lean is not different. Given the complexity of healthcare processes, delivering value on demand without waste can only occur by linking RIEs in a given VS.

The application of key Lean tools in the disciplined structure enables the organization to create prioritization and alignment, to see waste and eliminate waste, to enhance quality, and to improve design. Cherry-picking only one or two Lean tools such as only doing 5S or only adding production boards will not enable the organization to achieve the outcomes that Toyota or other truly Lean organizations have achieved.

A large cadre of Black Belts creates leavening for institutional transformation and enables daily elimination of the many small wastes that accompany all processes. Training Black Belts invests in your managers and creates a pipeline of Lean-trained individuals for future promotion. Having the senior executives, the physician, nursing and administrative leaders, and the middle managers trained appears ideal. Training below the level of middle managers appeared to us to yield less, probably because of the smaller span of control that is available to individuals below that level. However, participation in Lean in other meaningful ways such as 5S and RIEs develops the entire workforce.

A group of Lean facilitators who devoted time, energy, and skill to the VSs enabled good preparation, follow-up, and pace. They also can oversee the management of the archived learning for those who come after. These individuals can become a pipeline for department management positions.

RIEs are indeed "a remarkable social invention" (Liker, 2004). They break down silos, de-emphasize hierarchy, turn all level of employees into problem solvers, and yield amazing results in a week. The RIEs are the steam engine of pace and the pace produces results.

Aggressive pace and widespread employee engagement accelerate the financial, quality, and human development results. Your sensei will tell you that the rate of your organization's improvement will be directly proportional to your pace (Koenigsaecker, 2009). We had 14 VSs with the goal of eight to ten RIEs per year (some VSs did not achieve this pace), 2,000 employees on over 400 RIEs over six years, and about 250 Black Belts by year seven. At this point the financial benefit reached over $50 million in one year and the quality metrics and employee engagement metrics were excellent, reflecting the best outcomes we had ever achieved. This underscores that large organizations that have one or two VSs and several RIEs per year will think Lean does not work when, in fact, they have not done the work of Lean. Although this seemed intense to us, this pace was slow in comparison to the manufacturing companies who had the most successful Lean journeys (Koenigsaecker, 2009).

The flip side of the aggressive pace is having patience. It does take time to learn Lean and have it become the way to do work. Moreover, our systems have become dysfunctional over many decades and unraveling all the dysfunctions takes time. Remember that it took more than three decades at Toyota with consistent application of the philosophy and tools by committed leaders to achieve their results and they are still improving (Cooper, 2011).

The A3 is an incredibly powerful tool for problem solving and communication. Our use of it beyond RIEs and VSs created a common language and a unified concept for thinking about issues. As John Shook (2008) has stated, "[It is] a structured process for creating problem-solvers."

Measurement, accountability, and transparency are the only way to know what is working and what is not. Without measurement there is no accountability. Without transparency there is no trust. It is difficult to have an organization embrace a radically different approach to problem solving if the leadership cannot show and share results. Moreover, the ongoing and direct involvement of the CEO in reviewing and following up on the metrics facilitates higher performance.

As with any discipline, teaching others both internal and external to the organization helped us learn. Nothing hones one's knowledge like preparing a lecture "as the expert" or answering a penetrating question that you had not considered. Those of us who have presented papers are well aware of this.

In a similar manner, applying for awards such as the Colorado Performance Excellence Award or the Shingo Prize made us organize our thinking regarding our Lean journey and reflect on our successes and our areas for improvement. Such reflection is a part of Toyota's journey. Moreover, just as writing a journal paper or a grant proposal crystallizes one's thinking on the subject so does the submission for awards. Also, just as the feedback from reviewers of papers or grants improves the final product, so does the independent review that accompanies major awards.

Although these factors contributed to our success, we could have improved our outcome in several ways. We would have benefited both in terms of learning and outcomes from a full-time sensei from the beginning of our journey.

At the beginning it would have been better for all senior leadership to have had more in-depth training on both the philosophy and the tools of Lean. There is a rich literature in both and availing ourselves of that literature would have better informed our journey. In fact, since the beginning of our Lean journey almost a decade ago, the Lean consulting group we worked with markedly increased the depth and breadth of their engagement model to address these two constraints.

We asked all executive staff to participate in two RIEs per year, however, we all would have benefited from greater hands-on learning. We had standard work for all our Lean efforts, but we should have followed it always without deviation. We would have benefited from earlier and regular use of takt time and cycle time measurements, more effective visual management, and the establishment of model flow cells.

Although we did have some publications and many presentations from our Lean work, and formed a Lean Academy, we could have been more diligent in sharing our journey along the way. There were so many successful efforts across all components of Denver Health that could have been shared in a variety of publications and forums. This could not only have contributed to the spread of Lean but also it would have been a human development tool. Because many employees did not have experience in these areas, some structured approach to facilitating this would have been beneficial.

Implementation of Lean requires patience and perseverance. Although the Lean philosophy is noble, the tools intuitive, and the results impressive, it is not an easy journey or a quick fix. In fact, even in industry, the majority of entities that start Lean are no longer doing it after five years. Frequently, this lapse in the Lean effort is the result of a leadership transition. Experienced sensei believe that it takes a minimum of a decade to embed Lean in the culture. Toyota's incredible tenacity and continued development of TPS reflects a deeply committed leadership to the philosophy and to their relentless pursuit of perfection.

We learned much on our Lean journey. Therefore, it may be helpful for any organization either starting or already engaged in the Lean journey to reflect on the lessons we have learned just as we have benefited from the journeys of others who came before us.

Womack, Jones, and Roos (1990) began their book, *The Machine that Changed the World*, with this statement: "In the process we have become convinced that the principles of Lean production can be applied equally in every industry across the globe and that conversion to Lean production will have a profound effect on human society—it will truly change the world." Our healthcare "world" is crying out for change. Lean may well be the powerful medicine it needs.

Appendix

TABLE A.1

Milestones in the Lean Journey

Year 0 (2003)

AHRQ grant to explore path to system transformation

Year 1 (2004)

Adoption of Lean as approach for achieving system transformation; first group of
  22 Black Belts trained

Year 2 (2005) First partial year of Lean Journey

Required two Black Belt projects per year

Transitioned from project mode to Black Belts using Lean day to day

Required Black Belts to participate in 2 RIEs per year

Conducted first rapid improvement event (RIE)

Hired outside consulting sensei

Five value streams established by CEO

Established pace of 1 RIE per month per value stream

Second group of Black Belts trained

Year 3 (2006) First full year of Lean journey

Standardized Black Belt reports

Required monthly Black Belt reports

Established monthly value stream steering committee

Established lean systems improvement (LSI) department

Appointed Director of LSI

Hired five Lean facilitators

Conducted first 2P/3Ps

Formation of metric group

Lean SharePoint Site established

First value stream with $1,000,000 cumulative impact

Year 4 (2007) Second full year of Lean journey

First formal transformation plan of care event

Expanded to 14 value streams

Hired two more facilitators

Sensei present for two "event weeks" per month

Established pace of eight RIEs per year per value stream

Universal use of A3 thinking

continued

TABLE A.1 (continued)

Milestones in the Lean Journey

Patients participate on RIEs
Vendors/external entities participate on RIEs
Brought Black Belt training in-house
Training of 50 BBs per year (in groups of 25)
Conducted first vertical value stream analysis

Year 5 (2008) Third full year of Lean journey
Began external training (site visits and Medical Lean Institute)

Year 6 (2009) Fourth full year of Lean journey
$30,000/year target for Black Belts
Black Belt SharePoint Site
Initiated full-time embedded sensei model
Award application for Colorado Performance Excellence
Monthly meeting with all VS sponsors, LSI, sensei, and CEO
First VS achieved $10,000,000 cumulative financial impact
Six value streams with $1,000,000 cumulative financial benefit

Year 7 (2010) Fifth full year of Lean journey
Transitioned Black Belt reports to every other month; submitted application for Shingo
  Prize

Year 8 (2011) Sixth full year of Lean journey
VS production boards in individual area's central conference room
Transitioned Black Belt reports to quarterly
Current Black Belts contribute to training of new Black Belts
Created position of senior Lean facilitator
Permitted two value streams in specific high-intensity areas
First VS achieved $20,000,000 cumulative financial benefit

Year 9 (2012) Seventh full year of Lean journey
Created position of assistant director of LSI
First value stream achieved $30,000,000 cumulative financial benefit
15 value streams with $1,000,000 cumulative financial benefit

Value Stream Steering Committee Meeting

Value Stream: _____ Executive Sponsor: _____ Facilitator: _____

Date: _____ Time: _____ Attendees: _____

Financial Target: _____ Financial Status: _____

Value Stream Metrics

Metrics	Frequency	Baseline	Target	Status

3 Events Forward

Event Title	Date	Process Owner	Team Lead	Team	A3	Metrics	Comments

Green: Team complete & scheduled
1st 3 boxes of A3 are complete
Clear reason for action
Metrics established (with baselines)

Yellow: Team incomplete
1st 3 boxes of A3 are incomplete
Scope is not clearly identified
Metrics are not completely established

Red: Team not identified
No clear reason for action
Metrics are not identified
No Executive approval or support

3 Events Back

Event Title	Date	Process Owner	Team Lead	Metric	Baseline	Target	Status	Comments
								30–60–90 Complete date date date
								30–60–90 Complete date date date
								30–60–90 Complete date date date

FIGURE A.1
VS meeting template.

Black Belt Submitting Report	
Title of Black Belt Report	
Department	
Category	
Requesting Finance Review	
Accounting Unit Impacted	
Primary Contact	
Reason for Action	
Current State	
Target State	
Lean Tools Utilized	
Process to be used for sustainment	
Start date of new process	
Start date of savings/potential revenue	
Anticipated potential monthly savings/revenue/resources	
Documentation to support claimed dollar savings	
Additional comments & attachments	
Date of Report	
Savings tied to a specific Value Stream?	
Black Belt #1	
Black Belt #2	
Black Belt #3	
Black Belt #4	
Black Belt #5	
Black Belt #6	

FIGURE A.2
Black Belt reporting template.

Event Date:
Today's Date:

<u>Topic</u>   <u>Presenter</u>

Metric

Metric	Baseline	Target	Metric Owner (Reports metric to Rachel Koch)

Answer the following questions for each component of standard work developed by the team:

    1. Is the standard work documented in writing?
    2. Signed off by appropriate managers and executive staff?
    3. Being adhered to?
    4. Require modification by the team?
    5. Has a point person been assigned to ensure all of the above?

Completion Plans: Cut and paste completion plans from event A3 and document below accordingly:

Item	Person Responsible	Date	Status

Visual Management for this event:
Production board posted?

Production control board "evergreen" (updated regularly)?

6S in this area sustained?

Are Gemba rounds occurring with executive sponsor?

FIGURE A.3
Template for 30-, 60-, 90-day RIE review.

References

Arthur, J. (2011). *Lean Six Sigma for Hospitals: Simple Steps to Fast, Affordable Flawless Healthcare.* New York: McGraw-Hill.

Berra, Y. with Kaplan, D. (2001). *When You Come to a Fork in the Road, Take It.* New York: MJF.

Biffl, W.L., Beno, M., Goodman, P., et al. (2011). "Leaning" the process of venous thromboembolism prophylaxis. *Jt Comm J Qual Patient Saf.* 37: 99–109.

Bremer, M. and McKibben, B. (2011). *Escape the Improvement Trap: Five Ingredients Missing in Most Improvement Recipes.* New York: CRC Press.

Chalice, R. (2007). *Improving Healthcare Using Toyota Lean Production Methods: 46 Steps for Improvement.* Milwaukee: ASQ Quality Press.

Collins, S., Robertson, R., Garber, T., and Doty, M. 2013. *Insuring the Future: Current Trends in Health Coverage and the Effects of Implementing the Affordable Care Act.* New York: Commonwealth Fund.

Commonwealth Fund Commission on a High Performing Health System. (2013). *Confronting Costs: Stabilizing U.S. Health Spending While Moving Toward a High Performing Health Care System.* New York: The Commonwealth Fund.

Commonwealth Fund Commission on a High Performing Health System. (2012). *Rising to the Challenge: Results from a Scorecard of Local Health System Performance.* New York: The Commonwealth Fund.

Commonwealth Fund Commission on a High Performing Health System. (2011). *Why Not the Best? Results from the National Scorecard on U.S. Health System Performance, 2011.* New York: The Commonwealth Fund.

Cooper, C. (2011). *The Little Book of Lean: The Basics.* Pittsburgh: Simpler Consulting, LP.

Fulghum, R. (2003). *All I Really Need to Know I Learned in Kindergarten.* New York: Ballantine.

Gabow, P.A., Albert, R., Kaufman, L., Wilson. M., and Eisert, S. (2008). A picture of health. *Industrial Engineer.* 40: 45–49.

Gabow, P.A., Eisert, S., Karkhanis, A., Knight, A., et al. (2005). Toolkit for Redesign in Healthcare. *Agency for Healthcare Research and Quality* Publication No. 05-0108-EF. 2005.

Galsworth, G.D. (1997). *Visual Systems: Harnessing the Power of a Visual Workplace.* New York: AMACOM.

Hafer, M. (2012). *Simpler Healthcare: Using Lean to Achieve Breakthrough Improvement in Safety, Quality, Access and Productivity.* Pittsburgh: Simpler Consulting, LP.

Hino, S. (2002, English copyright 2006). *Inside the Mind of Toyota: Management Principles for Enduring Growth.* New York: Productivity Press.

IOM (Institute of Medicine). (2013). *Best Care at Lower Cost: Path to Continuously Learning Health Care in America.* Washington, DC: National Academies Press.

IOM (Institute of Medicine). (1999). *To Err is Human: Building a Safer Health System.* Washington, DC: National Academy Press.

Jackson, T.L. (2006). *Hoshin Kanri for the Lean Enterprise.* Boca Raton, FL: CRC Press.

Jimmerson, C. (2007). *A3 Problem Solving for Healthcare: A Practical Method for Eliminating Waste.* New York: Healthcare Performance Press.

Joint Commission Resources. (2008). *Advance Lean Thinking: Proven Methods to Reduce Waste and Improve Quality in Health Care.* Oakbrook Terrace, IL: Joint Commission Resources, Inc.

Joint Commission Resources. (2006). *Doing More with Less: Lean Thinking and Patient Safety in Healthcare.* Oakbrook Terrace, IL: Joint Commission Resource, Inc.

Juran, J.M. (1975). "The non-Pareto principle: Mea culpa" *Quality Progress.* 8(5): 8–9.

Kaiser Family Foundation accessed 1/5/2014.

Kanal, E., Borgstede, J.P., Barkovich, A.J., et al., (2002). American College of Radiology White Paper on MR Safety. *AJR.* 78: 1335–1347.

Keehan, S.P., Sisko, A.M., Truffer, A., et al. (2011). National health spending projections through 2020: Economic recovery and reform drive faster spending. *Health Aff.* 30(8): 1594–1605.

Kenny, C. (2011). *Transforming Health Care: Virginia Mason Medical Center's Pursuit of the Perfect Patient Experience.* New York: CRC Press.

Koenigsaecker, G. (2013). *Leading the Lean Enterprise Transformation,* second edition. New York: CRC Press.

Koenigsaecker, G. (2009). *Leading the Lean Enterprise Transformation.* New York: CRC Press.

Kulling, M. (2012). *Going Up! Elisha Otis's Trip to the Top.* Plattsburgh, NY: Tundra.

Liker, J.K. (2004). *The Toyota Way: 14 Management Principles from the World's Greatest Manufacturer.* New York: McGraw-Hill.

Litvak, E. and Fineberg, H.V. (2013). Smoothing the way to high quality, safety and economy. *N Engl J Med.* 369(17): 1581–1583.

Marchwinski, C., Shook, J., and Schroeder, A. (Eds.) (2008). *Lean Lexicon: A Graphic Glossary for Lean Thinkers.* Cambridge, MA: Lean Enterprise Institute.

McGlynn, E.A., Asch, S.M., Adams, J., et al. (2003). The quality of healthcare delivered to adults in the United States. *N Engl J Med.* 348(26): 2635–2645.

Michota, F.A. (Dec 2007. Epub Sep 22, 2007). Bridging the gap between evidence and practice in venous thromboembolism prophylaxis: The quality improvement process. *J Gen Intern Med.* 22(12): 1762–1770.

Miller, K. (2013). *We Don't Make Widgets: Overcoming the Myths that Keep Government from Radically Improving.* Washington, DC: Governing Books.

Moldenhauer, K., Sabel, A., Chu, E.S., and Mehler, P.S. (2009). Clinical triggers: An alternative to a rapid response team. *Jt Comm J Qual Patient Saf.* 35: 164–174.

O'Connor, M., Spinks, C., Mestas, T., and Sabel, A., et al. (2010). "Dyading" in the pediatric clinic improves access to care. *Clin Pediatr.* 49: 664–670.

Osada, T. (1991). *The 5S's: Five Keys to a Total Quality Environment.* Tokyo: Asian Productivity Organization.

Plsek, P. (2014). *Accelerating Health Care Transformation with Lean and Innovation: The Virginia Mason Experience.* Boca Raton, FL: CRC Press.

Productivity Press Development Team. (1996). *5S for Operators: 5 Pillars of the Visual Work Place.* New York: Productivity Press.

Robinson, J., Vastola, J., and Bookman, S. (2012). Doing more with less: Applying Lean methodology to EMS. *JEMS,* 37: 72–75.

Rother, M. and Shook, J. (2003). *Learning to See: Value-Stream Mapping to Create Value and Eliminate Muda.* Cambridge, MA: Lean Enterprise Institute.

Shook, J. (2008). *Managing to Learn: Using the A3 Management Process to Solve Problems, Gain Agreement, Mentor and Learn.* Cambridge, MA: The Lean Enterprise Institute.

Toussaint, J. and Gerard, R.A., with Adams, E. (2010). *On the Mend: Revolutionizing Healthcare to Save Lives and Transform the Industry.* Cambridge, MA: Lean Enterprise Institute.

Toussaint, J. and Gruner, D. (2013). Beyond the CEO: Sustaining ThedaCare's culture. Paper presented at annual Institute of Healthcare Improvement Forum, Orlando, FL.

UHC Clinical Data Base/Resource Manager. Chicago, IL, 2007–2012. http://www.uhc.edu

Womack, J.P. and Jones, D.T. (2003). *Lean Thinking: Banish Waste and Create Wealth in Your Corporation.* New York: Free Press.

Womack, J.P., Jones, D.T., and Roos, D. (1990). *The Machine that Changed the World.* New York: Rawson Associates, Scribner Simon and Schuster.

World Bank. (2014). *Data Catalog GDP Ranking.* Accessed Jan 5, 2014.

Index